If Grace Is True

If Grace Is True

Why God Will Save Every Person

Philip Gulley
James Mulholland

HarperOne
An Imprint of HarperCollinsPublishers

HarperOne

HarperCollins books may be purchased for educational, business, or sales promotional use. For information, please e-mail the Special Markets Department at SPsales@harpercollins.com.

Designed by Joseph Rutt

HarperCollins Web site: http://www.harpercollins.com
HarperCollins®, h®, and HarperOne™ are
trademarks of HarperCollins Publishers.

FIRST HARPERCOLLINS PAPERBACK EDITION
PUBLISHED IN 2004

Library of Congress Cataloging-in-Publication Data
is available upon request.

ISBN 978–0–06–192608–2

15 16 17 RRD(C) 10 9 8 7 6

Dedications

To my father, who taught me
to ask questions.
To Joe Jones, who taught me
to ask questions about God.
To my aunt Nancy, who taught me
to ask questions fearlessly.
James Mulholland

To my wife, Joan, and my sons,
Spencer and Sam.
Philip Gulley

Acknowledgments

This book took three years to write. It was an often painful process full of fits and starts. It tested and ultimately deepened our friendship. It challenged our beliefs and lifestyles. There were moments when we nearly lost our courage. Not everyone has supported us. Fortunately, throughout these three years, God raised up people to cheer us on.

Our gracious wives, Joan and Angie, allowed us the time and space to think and write. Our two Quaker meetings, Fairfield and Irvington, have defended and supported their heretical pastors. Countless friends read parts of the manuscript along the way and offered helpful comments and penetrating critique. Royal Mulholland, Gloria Gulley, John Shonle, Julia Roller, Roger Freet,

Acknowledgments

Malcolm Herring, Nancy Sanders, Kathy and Duane Rosenberg, Chris Wynn, Cathy Gibson, Tom Davis, Harold Miller, Jennifer Custer, and Joe Jones all encouraged our writing.

We've had the good fortune of claiming Steve Hanselman as our editor. Steve has believed in this project from the beginning, stood with us through the doubts and opposition, and pushed us to create a better book. To him, and those like him, who dare to believe in the scandalous grace of God, we are grateful.

Phil and Jim

Contents

A Note from the Authors

We've been friends since we stood in line together at registration for our first year of seminary. We sat next to each other in class, pastored small city churches, edited each other's sermons, and struggled together with the complexities of knowing and serving God. We deeply treasure the friendship God has given us. The book you are about to read is the fruit of that relationship.

Certain risks are inherent in coauthoring a book, even for the best of friends. Chief among them are the differences of opinion that arise in thinking and writing about the most personal of life's dimensions—the spiritual. Fortunately, as we wrote this book, we marveled at the many points at which our theology agreed. Though our backgrounds differ, our experiences with God are remarkably alike. Over time, it seemed quite natural to write as one voice. Hence, this book, though authored by two people, is written in the first person.

There are pragmatic reasons for writing this book in one voice. It seemed awkward to use the word *we* or to distinguish continually between "Phil" and "Jim." Some of the stories in this book come from Phil's life, some from Jim's, and some are a combination of similar encounters. Regardless, they represent our shared view of life. We also hoped not identifying the author of a given passage would provide additional anonymity for the people we've written about. To that end, we've changed the names of most people to mask their identity further.

However, the chief reason we wrote this book together arises from our belief that theology is a conversation, not a monologue. We committed ourselves to writing a book both of us could fully affirm. That wasn't always easy, but we believe this book is better and truer for our having worked together than if we had toiled alone. In that same spirit of Christian community, we invite your thoughtful response to the issues we've raised. Though we might not be able to respond personally to every contribution, we will take it seriously.

Though we realize a book of this nature is sure to generate disagreement and even hostility, our hope is

A Note from the Authors

that it will help our readers experience God's grace and presence in a deeper way. To that end, we offer this book to you, the reader, praying God's gracious Spirit might use it to bless and enrich your life.

Philip Gulley and
James Mulholland

One

The Dilemma

Sally was likely dead before she hit the floor. One minute she was laughing with co-workers. The next minute she lay crumpled at their feet. They called the paramedics, who rushed her forty miles to the hospital, where the doctors and nurses kept her heart beating for twelve more hours. Long enough for her son to call the church and ask me to come. Time enough for family to gather, to grieve, and to ask why. The doctor called it a stroke. I called it a mystery. Neither answer brought much comfort. Whatever the explanation, Sally was likely dead before she hit the floor.

Sally's death shook me. She was my age, our birthdays only a week apart. I thought this the cause of my discomfort when they asked me to speak at her funeral, but in preparing her eulogy I faced far more than my own mortality. I learned many secrets about this woman whom I'd often judged, sometimes condemned, and never respected. I discovered her life had been as cruel as her death. I realized my opinion of Sally had been unfair. At her funeral, I would bury my self-righteousness and arrogance. I would leave next to the flowers arranged around her grave a belief I'd held since I was a child.

Let me tell you about Sally.

Sally's father deserted her when she was three. Her mother filled the void with a parade of temporary replacements, none of whom wanted Sally underfoot. She was discarded. Passed from aunt to cousin to grandmother and back again, staying only as long as their patience allowed. Shuffled from school to school, from town to town. She made only acquaintances, never a friend. Longing for a stability she'd never known, Sally married young, and poorly.

Her husband abandoned her with three small children, no job, and no diploma. Her dreams withered away as she struggled to survive. All her life she'd been neglected, and now she began to neglect herself. Like dominoes falling, bad jobs were followed by worse ones; a poor husband was replaced by abusive boyfriends. Alcohol and drugs sped her descent. When the last domino toppled, Sally was thirty-two years old, the mother of five, unemployed, and living off the leftovers of neighbors and relatives. That domino tumbled the day she slept in with a hangover and woke to find her youngest daughter drowned in the pool next door.

When her son came and through his tears told me the news, I could barely contain my rage. Unaware of Sally's sad past, I saw only a mother who had failed her child, and I despised her. It was with great difficulty that I preached her daughter's funeral.

Before the funeral, Sally told me she'd been abandoned by God. I assured her God hadn't forsaken her. I told her, "God loves you. He knows your pain. You're not alone." But I offered those words through gritted teeth, certain she neither heard nor cared and doubting, myself, whether in her case it was true.

After the funeral Sally stood by her daughter's casket, clutching a wad of tissue and crying. "There's no reason to live," she said. "No reason at all."

She was wrong.

The last five years of Sally's life were her happiest. That's what everyone said at Sally's funeral. That's what her children said, what her mother said, what her friends said—Sally's last five years were her best.

How could that be?

In the days after her daughter's death, Sally repented. Now by *repentance,* I don't mean she fell to her knees at a church altar and confessed her sins aloud. I don't mean she affirmed a set of spiritual laws or accepted a Lord and Savior. By *repentance,* I simply mean what the word itself means—Sally turned. She turned from thoughts of suicide. She turned from crippling self-pity. She turned from despair. She turned.

Sally moved to a small town. She found a job. Then she found a better one. She bought a car. She bought a house. She planted flowers. She even planted a tree. She made friends, not acquaintances. She made peace with her family. Life wasn't perfect, but she'd turned from despair.

A month before her death, she told her son of a new and surprising desire. The day before Sally's funeral, her son revealed her confession to me. It was the memory that comforted him the most. His mother had simply confided, "I think I'm going to look for a church."

Sally died searching.

The woman I'd so easily disregarded while she lived had become a dilemma in her death. I sat in my office, reflecting on all I had learned and struggling with the words I should speak at Sally's funeral. To many Christians, Sally's destiny was an easy judgment. Having never accepted Christ, Christ wouldn't accept her. She was doomed to hell.

I grew up believing we were destined for either heaven or hell. I was taught that only those who confessed their sins and accepted Jesus as their Savior before they died would live with God forever. All the rest would suffer hell's eternal torment. As a child, I'd never questioned this formula. It was simple and clear. As an adult, I'd held on to this belief despite life's complexities.

Now Sally's life and death had unsettled what was once a sure conviction. In clear response to our prayers, she had been drawing close to God. She'd turned from the path of destruction. She'd been asking, seeking, and knocking. I couldn't believe God would invite Sally to his home, then slam the door as she stood at the threshold. It seemed a cruel joke.

What should I say at Sally's funeral?

I was torn. I'd once thought hell a fitting end to her life. But when I learned more about her, that judgment troubled me. Sally had spent her life climbing out of hell. How could I wish for her return? Though it defied the formula I'd been taught, I wanted God to be gracious to Sally. My scorn gave way to sympathy.

I began to pray, asking God to welcome Sally to heaven, to make a way for her to experience the truth of what I'd told her. "God loves you. He knows your pain. You're not alone." I thought about that for a while. The longer I thought, the clearer the answer became.

God loved Sally far more than I. He'd been there when she cried herself to sleep as a little girl, when she was abused and rejected by those around her, when her efforts to find happiness led only to more misery, and when in her moment of greatest despair she determined to keep trying. If the little I knew had changed my heart toward Sally, why was it so hard to believe God was even more gracious? It was the formula. It limited God's grace.

The next day at the funeral, instead of talking about the formula, I spoke of grace. I read a story Jesus told—a story of a father and his prodigal son, of a son who wandered afar before turning toward home, of a father waiting, hoping, and longing.

I said, "Some people think God sits on a throne, holding fast to holiness and justice, waiting for us to grovel at his feet. But last night, as I thought about Sally, I remembered another prodigal's homecoming. I realized God is never content to wait on his throne. God was standing at the door watching for Sally, just as surely as that father watched for his prodigal. And while she was yet at a distance, God saw her and had compassion. God ran and embraced her. God welcomed her home."

In the telling, I knew it to be true.

That night I sat in my living room thinking back on Sally's funeral. It had been a good funeral. Sally's family said my words about her rang true. A good funeral not only should speak the truth about the person, it should ring true about God. It should speak of a Father who does not abandon his children. Even the Sallys of our world. Especially the Sallys.

A good funeral should also speak of grace. Now by *grace,* I don't mean an expected reward earned by good people. Neither do I mean a divine gift offered grudgingly to a chosen few. I don't mean any notion that slips easily and naturally into our tidy formulas. By *grace,* I mean God's unfailing commitment to love.

Writing Sally's eulogy was the breaching of a dam—the first rivulet of what would soon become a coursing flood. For many years God had been eroding my obsessive devotion to judgment, punishment, and wrath. God had used countless experiences to wear away my inadequate understanding of his grace. The life and stories of Jesus had slowly undercut theological formulas I'd accepted uncritically. Sally's funeral simply washed away any remnants of resistance. The dam ruptured, and grace swept through, softening ground that had long been cracked and dry.

Now I have a new formula. It too is simple and clear. It is the most compelling truth I've ever known. It is changing my life. It is changing how I talk about God. It is changing how I think about myself. It is changing how I treat other people. It brings me untold joy, peace, and hope. This truth is the best news I've ever heard, ever believed, and ever shared.

I believe God will save every person.

Now by *salvation,* I mean much more than a ticket to heaven. I mean much more than being cleansed of our sins and rescued from hell's fire. I mean even more than being raised from the grave and granted eternal life. By *salvation,* I mean being freed of every obstacle to intimacy with God. We will know as we are known and love as we are loved.

Some have already experienced this salvation, though not all call it by that name. Others, like Sally, long for this salvation but will find it only beyond the grave. Many, like me, have experienced God's love but have misunderstood salvation. We've thought it a trophy rather than a gift, a personal achievement rather than a work of God. We've gloried in our salvation and damned those whose obstacles have far exceeded our own.

I was ungracious to Sally. There were so few hurdles in my life. I was blessed with good parents, a nurturing church, a loving wife, healthy children, education, and affluence. I'd known love as long as I could remember. My sin was comparing Sally to myself and despising her. She faced difficulties I'll never understand.

I do understand her reluctance to believe God loved her. Though my religious experience was largely positive, I often vacillated between reveling in God's favor and fearing God's wrath. I'd been told of God's love, but warnings of God's high expectation and the consequences of failure were equally emphasized. Sunday school tales of Adam and Eve's ejection, the flood's destruction, and God's quick retribution for the slightest infraction only reinforced my fears. Lot's wife took one look back and was turned into a pillar of salt. I spent my early years afraid I'd displease God with my thoughts, words, or actions and he'd destroy me.

Fortunately, Sunday school also introduced me to Jesus, who became a friend and companion, forgiving and understanding. I easily accepted his divinity. He became the focus of my prayers and adoration. I knew Jesus loved me because the Bible told me so. The biblical accounts of God's attitude weren't as comforting. Hearing that Jesus was all that stood between me and God's wrath didn't ease my anxiety. God wanted to destroy me, but Jesus had died for me. I found myself wishing God could be more like Jesus. At Sally's funeral, I realized he was.

The grace I experienced in Jesus was the grace of God. The Father he spoke of—who welcomed the prodigal and embraced Sally—was the very Father who loved me. The assurance of this love freed me from childhood fears, enabling me to voice these optimistic words: *I believe God will save every person.*

Seven words. Seven simple words. When I first spoke them in a sermon, I stated them boldly, hoping for agreement. Some folks were intrigued, but others were appalled. Some even suggested I had abandoned my faith. They all had questions. Good questions. Thoughtful questions.

"How can you contradict thousands of years of tradition and the testimony of the Bible?"

"Of course, God is love, but isn't he also holy and just?"

"Aren't we free to reject God's love and ignore his grace?"

"If everyone is going to heaven, why was Jesus necessary?"

"You mean even Adolph Hitler will be in heaven?"

I've prayed and thought about these questions. I'll address them further on. But these questions have not diminished my conviction: I believe God will save every person.

This book is about those seven words.

T w o

Trusting Our Experience with God

I believe God will save every person.

Those aren't easy words to accept. Especially, if like me, you grew up believing some would be saved and most would be damned. It took many years for my belief to change. God had to overcome my objections. I resisted because such extravagant grace wasn't the traditional teaching of the Church. It wasn't the usual interpretation of Scripture. It wasn't the formula I'd been taught as a child. My belief changed only as I recognized the grace I'd experienced was not limited or conditional. I know a God of boundless love.

I've never experienced a God of wrath. I've heard such a God preached. I've read of such a God. I've encountered wrathful people who claimed to be acting on

God's behalf. I've even allowed such sentiments to tarnish my view of God. Yet, in the midst of all these distortions, I never experienced a wrathful God.

The God I've experienced is the God of Jesus—a God of unlimited patience, infinite love, and eternal faithfulness. Jesus described a God who waits long through the night, with the light lit and the door open, confident his most defiant child will one day realize his love and turn toward home. Jesus revealed a God who loves the unlovable, touches the untouchable, and redeems those thought beyond redemption. He said, "As the Father has loved me, so have I loved you" (John 15:9). My earliest experiences were with the love of Jesus.

When I was a teenager, I went with a friend to a concert at the inner-city Pentecostal church he attended. The music was unremarkable, at times even dreadful, leaving me unusually grateful when the pastor stood to deliver a sermon. I'll never forget his message. Though his words were brief, their effect was enduring. He recalled the ministry of Jesus, how time and again Jesus had loved, healed, and forgiven broken, sinful people.

While I was familiar with all his examples, and easily could have dismissed his message as the same old story, I didn't. Instead, in that small, inner-city Pentecostal church, in the third row from the front, I responded to Jesus.

At the end of his message, the minister invited people who wished to accept Jesus to come forward to the altar. I hesitated, concerned what others might think of me. I'd gone to church all my life. Would they think me a fraud? Worse, I was afraid I might begin speaking in tongues or break into dancing. In my religious tradition, these were not signs of the Spirit, but of mental instability. Yet in that moment, the love of Jesus was such an attraction, I couldn't resist. I had to know this love more deeply. Nothing could keep me from it—not my pride, not even my religious tradition. I rose from my seat and went forward.

My experience is not unique. Many testify to the power of the Jesus story. In ways we don't fully understand and can't completely communicate, we were drawn to Jesus. *And yet not to Jesus alone.* It was the God of Jesus that attracted us. The God who loves people more than formulas, mercy more than judgment, and pardon more than punishment. The God who seeks the lost, heals the brokenhearted, accepts the outcast, is kind to the wicked and ungrateful, is merciful and forgiving, and loves the whole world.

Many share my love for Jesus. We accepted him as Lord. We were baptized in his name. We became his disciples. We worshiped and adored him. Yet we've often divorced the words and actions of Jesus from the God he worshiped and adored. We've forgotten the very one Jesus came to reveal.

Those of us raised in the Church have a good excuse for this confusion. It's what we were taught. The church of my childhood often glorified Jesus at God's expense. Jesus was Savior. God was judge and executioner. Jesus was closer than a brother. God was distant—remote at best and hostile at worst. Many churches fail to emphasize that the love we experience in Jesus is the persistent grace of God.

Nevertheless, on that night in a little Pentecostal church, I couldn't say no. I could no more reject this love than a man dying of thirst could refuse a cup of water. The attraction was so powerful I couldn't understand why the altar didn't fill with people. I was so enthralled with this gracious God I eventually became a pastor. I wanted to spend my life helping people experience God's love. Most pastors, regardless of their theology, share my passion. We retell the stories of Jesus because we're convinced if people catch even a glimpse of God's heart, they'll respond. We believe that when people turn toward God his grace will ultimately overcome every obstacle.

In my first pastorate I was certain if I could preach the perfect sermon the altar would fill with people overcome by God's grace. Now I realize there are many hindrances to experiencing the fullness of God's grace—confusion, fear, prejudice, ignorance, and pride, to name a few. The removal of these obstacles ought to be the primary purpose of the Church.

Unfortunately, the Church has often erected more barriers than we've removed. Too many have entered our doors, only to experience condemnation rather than welcome. We've acted less like Jesus and more like his opponents. I wonder if Sally's fragile faith would have survived such a cold reception. Would she have given up her search when the people of God lacked the compassion of God?

Or would Sally's experience have been like mine? Despite the Church's failings, she might have found herself drawn to Jesus and overwhelmed by the love of God. She might have learned what I've learned—that intimacy with God is not about joining a church. It's not about knowing your religion's doctrines, tenet by tenet. It's not about knowing your holy writings, backward and forward, in their original language. It's not about knowing God as a theory or abstraction. Intimacy with God is more like making love than joining a club, hearing a lecture, or reading a book. There are simply some things we must experience for ourselves.

Experiences with God aren't limited to church altars. Many experiences aren't connected to Jesus. I've encountered God's grace in the most surprising places. Sitting around a campfire and watching the stars. Standing on a beach as a storm rolled in. Having my friends gather at my house during a tragedy. A letter of encouragement arriving on a day I'd decided to quit. God delights in taking such common experiences and filling them with his presence. The more I have experienced this love, the more I am persuaded God extends such a grace to every person, not just me.

One such instance occurred on the street outside the apartment where my wife and I were living. I was in a 1974 VW Beetle with torn seats and holes in the floor-board. It was winter. The day was gray and bitter cold. The heater in my car didn't work. I eased up to the curb, careful to park so I could get out without having to put the car in reverse, which no longer worked. I turned off the engine, gathered my college textbooks from the seat beside me, and in that moment was filled with joy. Truthfully, *joy* is too small a word to describe how I felt.

Sitting there in my VW Beetle, I knew two things: God loved me—desperately, achingly loved me—and all would be well. I knew even if I flunked out of college, even if my car broke down, even if my marriage failed, even if no church would have me as their pastor, I was unconditionally loved.

I realize how easily such experiences can be dis-counted. They sound silly even to me. I wish I could tell you of something more spectacular—of an angelic visit, of writing on the wall, of a blinding light and a voice from heaven. Though my experiences with God have been compelling for me, some will explain them away as youthful enthusiasm or emotional weakness. One person's epiphany is another person's triviality. When Paul saw Jesus in a blinding light on the road to Damascus, his companions saw nothing.

These experiences didn't immediately convince me of God's universal love. Only gradually did I suspect God loved everyone as deeply as God loved me. It might have been easier if on the night before Sally's funeral God had appeared to me and said, "Don't worry. Sally's with me." I used to wish God would be so forthright, but I've come to value his subtle leading. I'm grateful he doesn't bludgeon us with his truth but leads us there tenderly, carefully, as we are able to hear it. Like Elijah, I thought God would speak in the wind or the earthquake or the fire, so when he whispered his truth I was caught unaware.

What I could not learn in the wind, earthquake, and fire, God taught me in his whispers: *I love you. You are mine. I will never leave nor forsake you.*

This is what he whispered as I rose from my pew in the Pentecostal church and sat shivering with joy in my car. It is what God has whispered ever since. When he first spoke those endearments, I remember thinking he probably said that to all his children. At Sally's funeral, I realized he does.

If grace is true, it is true for everyone.

It is really as simple as that. In this book, I'll explain the reasons I believe God will save every person. I'll talk about what it means if God is love and grace is true. I'll assert God's will is the redemption of the whole world. I'll proclaim how in Jesus grace was lived, tested, and triumphant. I'll share my conviction that grace persists beyond the grave. But I need to admit my faith is not based primarily on theological reasoning. I believe because God whispered in my ear.

I'm hoping you've also experienced this God of grace. Perhaps you've encountered him through Jesus or have known God's grace by other names. If not, you may find my stories and ideas ridiculous. But if you've known those moments of unexpected bliss, I hope you'll ponder what such moments say about God's attitude toward you and toward everyone else.

I didn't consider this for many years. I actually thought my experiences rare. I was one of the chosen. I was special. Now I know the truth. God whispers his love in every ear. He isn't interested in declaring his love to a select few. He doesn't limit his presence to Vatican City, to the halls of seminaries, to the offices of preachers, or to church altars. God doesn't restrict his communication to the Bible. He doesn't confine his presence to any single denomination or religion. God speaks to all people, even when they're not inclined to listen.

Fortunately, God looks for the slightest yielding, the smallest opening, to make his love known. God doesn't stand with his back turned until we ask for him. God doesn't hide and expect us to seek him. God doesn't keep his distance and await our call. God said, "I revealed myself to those who did not ask for me; I was found by those who did not seek me. To a nation that did not call on my name, I said, 'Here I am, here I am'" (Isaiah 65:1). What God did for the children of Israel, God does for all. God stands at the door and knocks, and if we don't answer, he looks for an open window.

My grandfather often told the story of how he and four teenage friends went to a revival intent on disrupting it by heckling the speaker and mocking the proceedings. Instead, he and his friends ended up at the altar. They hadn't attended the revival to find God. They went as a prank. Yet God responded to their disrespect not with wrath but with grace. While my grandfather and his friends might not have been interested in knowing God, God was interested in knowing them.

Just as God longed to be known by those teenagers, he longs to be known by all. I'm not the first to believe this. The prophet Jeremiah made it clear that the salvation of every person was not merely God's desire, it was his promise.

> "The time is coming," declares the Lord, "when I will make a new covenant with the house of Israel and with the house of Judah. . . . I will put my law in their minds and write it on their hearts. I will be their God and they will be my people. No longer will a man teach his neighbor, or a man his brother, saying, 'Know the Lord,' because they will *all* know me. From the least of them to the greatest. For I will forgive their wickedness and will remember their sins no more." (Jeremiah 31:31–34)

Jeremiah spoke thousands of years ago what I have only recently discovered: we will all know God. God has resolved to forgive our wickedness and remember our sins no more. He has determined to write his way on our minds and in our hearts. We shall all be cleansed by his mercy and transformed by his grace.

It was no accident the early Church claimed Jeremiah's vision as the promise Jesus came to fulfill *and expand*—a new covenant, written not on stone but on every human heart. Early Christians announced God's yearning to be known by all—Jew and Greek, male and female, slave and free. Though Jeremiah's vision stopped at Israel's gate, Jesus declared God's saving love for those outside the gate. He reminded them, "I have other sheep that are not of this sheep pen, I must bring them also" (John 10:16). He said, "When I am lifted up from the earth, I will draw *all* men to myself" (John 12:32). What John claimed for Jesus, Jesus claimed for God.

I often wonder how I missed this ultimate triumph of grace. For years, though I proclaimed Christianity as the fulfillment of God's covenant, I completely ignored what was promised—God's intention to draw all people to himself. I suppose I was one of those who Jesus said "had eyes but couldn't see and ears but couldn't hear." I failed to listen to the voice of God, especially when what he whispered seemed so scandalous, so outside my tidy formulas. Fortunately, God persisted.

Sally's funeral, my epiphany in my VW Beetle, and my evening at the Pentecostal church are only a few of the experiences that have led me to believe God will fulfill his promise. In this book, I'll share many more. These experiences with God have become the bedrock of my faith. I trust them.

You may think me foolish to trust my experiences and to question beliefs held for thousands of years by millions of sincere people. I was initially uneasy believing something other than what I'd been taught. How could I justify what ran counter to certain Scriptures? Then I remembered another man who faced my dilemma.

This man trusted his experience with God even though it challenged a belief of his religion and contradicted certain Scriptures. His experience with God would lead him to reject the formulas he and his friends had cherished. He was compelled to believe in a grace far greater than he had ever imagined. His story has given me the courage to believe something new.

A Man Called Peter

His parents named him Simon. Jesus, recognizing Simon's fierce loyalty and stubborn persistence, nicknamed him Peter—the Rock. Unfortunately, rocks are not known for their flexibility. Though Jesus taught Peter many things, it took a vision from God to alter his beliefs.

In the tenth chapter of Acts, we're told Peter saw the heavens open and a sheet descend from the sky. The sheet contained certain creatures the Scriptures forbid Peter, a faithful Jew, to eat. The voice of God said, "Rise, Peter, kill and eat."

Peter replied, "No, Lord; for I have never eaten any-thing that is common or unclean" (Acts 10:13–14, RSV).

Peter knew what he believed. He was faithful to those beliefs, even if it meant saying no to God. Then again, *no* is almost always our first response to God. Especially when God wants us to think or act in a new way.

Like most of us, Peter was resistant to change. God had to repeat the vision twice. During each vision, Peter was cautioned not to reject what God had accepted. While Peter puzzled about his visions, God sent three Gentile men to knock on his door.

To appreciate how Peter felt when he saw them on his doorstep, you need only recall your discomfort when unwelcome visitors knock on your door. Multiply that by ten. Three times Peter had been told to accept what he considered unacceptable. Now three Gentiles stood at his door.

Peter opened the door.

The men asked Peter to accompany them to the house of Cornelius, a Gentile. Peter was torn. To visit a Gentile's home was to violate the rigid rules separating Jew from Gentile. Rubbing shoulders with Gentiles wasn't kosher. Socializing with them was fraternizing with the enemy. Torn between what he'd always been taught and his experience with God, Peter relied on his experience. He went with the men and saw God pour out his Spirit on the house of Cornelius and all the Gentiles gathered there.

Peter rejected what he'd learned at his father's knee. He rejected what his rabbi had taught. He rejected what his friends believed. He trusted his experience with God, though it challenged a belief of his religion and contradicted certain Scriptures. Despite all this pressure to conform, Peter believed something new.

I'd read Peter's story countless times. Only when I began to consider the salvation of every person did I appreciate his courage in believing something new. We're all resistant to a new belief, especially when that belief requires us to accept people we've long considered unacceptable. Peter's vision represented a seismic shift in the popular understanding of God's grace. Such shifts unsettle the world. It unsettled Peter's world.

Consider how difficult those days must have been for him. It's not easy to believe and act in opposition to your religious tradition. It earns you few friends and many enemies. In the eleventh chapter of Acts, Peter faced severe criticism from other disciples of Jesus for asserting God's grace was *even* for me, a Gentile.

We often forget the first followers of Jesus were Jewish. Some of these disciples believed God's grace was for the Jew alone. They developed formulas that limited

Philip Gulley and James Mulholland

God's grace to those who were circumcised, kept dietary laws, and essentially became Jewish. Peter voiced another view. He trusted his experience with God and believed in a more extravagant grace.

Peter discovered God's grace was never intended to bless only a few. When he saw Gentiles experiencing the grace he'd experienced, he said, "I now realize how true it is that God does not show favoritism, but accepts men from every nation who fear him and do what is right" (Acts 10:34).

This radical grace shouldn't have surprised him. The Hebrew Scriptures abound with hints of God's love for all people. Indeed, God's first words to Abraham include the promise, "*All* peoples on earth will be blessed through you" (Genesis 12:3). Peter knew he could no longer believe God's grace was limited to the Jew.

I believe in an even more extravagant grace.

This shouldn't surprise you. The Christian Scriptures teem with promises of God's abundant grace. Indeed, Jesus was seen as a fulfillment of Isaiah's prophecy that "*all* mankind will see God's salvation" (Luke 3:6). I no longer believe God's grace is limited to the Christian. I don't believe God's grace is limited at all.

Of course, I haven't always believed this. There was a time when I limited God's grace to Christians and defined *Christian* as anyone who closely resembled me.

25

While I had experienced God's grace, I had also been taught a set of beliefs and an interpretation of Scripture that required the damnation of those who did not believe as I believed. The conflict between my experience and these beliefs raged for many years. This is why Peter's story was so helpful to me. It encouraged me to base my faith on my experiences with God.

I remain thankful for the rich tradition of the Church and for the powerful words of Scripture. I am indebted to those who introduced me to Jesus, his words, and his example. I am also grateful I've been freed from my need to confine God within the boundaries of my tradition and my interpretations of Scripture. I appreciate the consistent manner in which Jesus pointed toward God. I've come to recognize that all religious truth is born of intimate experiences with God. Belief and Scripture are the offspring of such experiences.

Experience and Belief

The summer before I went to college my mother knit me a sweater. It was a thick Technicolor kind of sweater with bright blues, purples, greens, and browns. It was ugly. I seldom wore it but treasured it because my mother had given it to me.

One day my wife went through our clothes in order to give some things we no longer wore to Goodwill. When I came home I found my mother's sweater on top of the pile. I was appalled! How could she throw away a sweater made by my mother? She pointed out I never wore the sweater. I pointed out it was a gift from my mother and put it back in my drawer.

Many years later my wife came home to find the sweater on top of a pile of clothes destined for the Salvation Army. She picked up the sweater and asked, "How can you throw away a sweater that was a gift from your mother?" I finally admitted it was ugly and I was too embarrassed to wear it.

It's always difficult to discard those things we once found meaningful. All of us can remember objects we held precious that eventually ended up in a garage sale or a trash bin. What we treasured was left behind. What is true in the material world is also the case in the spiritual journey. Often it's necessary to discard once-cherished beliefs in order to be faithful to our experiences with God. Leaving old beliefs behind is always painful.

It's helpful to remember we weren't born with beliefs. Peter wasn't born believing Gentiles were outside God's grace. I wasn't born believing some people would spend eternity in hell. We were taught what to believe. Some of what we were taught was reinforced by our experiences with God, but much we accepted with little thought or reflection. If those in authority said it, it must be true.

I'm not sure when Peter first eyed his Gentile neighbors with suspicion and scorn. I do remember when I began to believe some people would spend eternity in hell. I was ten years old when our church held a revival. The evangelist strode back and forth across the platform, describing in exquisite detail the torments of hell—the sizzling flesh, the murderous thirst, the unceasing torture, the absence of God.

The evangelist warned, "Tonight, on your way home, you could be hit by a train and be eternally damned to hell."

I remember my deep relief that there were no railroad tracks between the church and my house.

When he finished preaching I was persuaded of two things: hell was real, and I didn't want to go there. I believed the evangelist because he spoke with passion. I believed him because he read about hell from the Bible. I believed him because most of the people were saying "Amen." Most of all, I believed him because I was a child.

Only as an adult did I realize how inconsistent this belief was with the God I was coming to know. Only as I matured was I able to find the confidence and courage to challenge this belief. Only as I experienced God's grace did I discover spiritual maturity came with the same painful growth necessary to every other sphere of life. If "Jesus grew in wisdom and stature, and in favor with God and men" (Luke 2:52), so must I.

One of the signs of maturity is when we stop believing everything we've been told. When I was in second grade, I stopped believing in Santa Claus. When I was in sixth grade, I stopped believing the opposite sex had cooties. When I was in high school, I stopped believing my parents knew everything.

Today, my father and I enjoy a wonderfully warm friendship. That was not always the case. As a teenager, I chafed under his rule. I would often question his authority. "Why?" I'd ask. "Because I said so, that's why!" he'd say. When I was a child, that answer sufficed, but the older I grew the more it rankled. When I was nineteen, I told my father his saying so didn't make it so.

Questioning my father was a necessary step in my maturity. I had reached that moment in my life when I believed my experience was as trustworthy as my father's experience. I was still willing to seek my father's counsel. I still loved my father deeply. It was simply the case that I no longer believed everything he believed. While much of what he'd said and taught turned out to be true, I found some of the ways my father viewed the world inconsistent with my experiences. During these years, I learned the importance of asking whether what I've been taught was true. Of course, that answer can be found only through experience.

I'm thankful for many of the beliefs I was taught. Without beliefs to guide us, making choices is nearly impossible. The problem is our tendency to carve our beliefs in stone. We too easily adopt uncompromising attitudes and replace once-cherished beliefs with a new collection of rigid assumptions. We forget life is a series of experiences that continually challenge the beliefs we hold sacred.

The prophet Isaiah wrote, "O Lord, you are our Father. We are the clay, and you are the potter; we are all the work of your hand" (Isaiah 64:8). Whenever I've carved my beliefs in stone I've hindered the work of God. I've allowed my initial experiences to alter my beliefs but too quickly assumed God's work with me was complete. It has taken powerful experiences to soften my heart and mind so I could be molded in new ways. Often these experiences have caused a crisis of faith.

Experience and Crisis

A crisis of faith is any experience that calls into question what we've accepted and believed about God. It is a moment when we are forced to ask the question *why?*

Peter's vision was such an experience. He was compelled to ask himself and others, "Why shouldn't God's grace extend to the Gentiles?"

Just as Peter had his crisis of faith, I had mine. It came as I wrote the words for Sally's funeral and had to wrestle with whether Sally had been abandoned by God. I was forced to ask myself, "Why shouldn't God's grace extend to Sally?"

I've learned that asking why is never being unfaithful. *Why* we believe is every bit as important as *what* we believe. I once focused on *what* I believed and gave little thought to *why* I believed it. My uncritical faith often failed when exposed to the light of experience. As my faith has matured I've become more willing to examine not only what I believe, but why I believe it, and to regularly test whether my beliefs match my experiences with God. "I've experienced it!" is the most compelling response to "Why do you believe that?"

When Peter stood before his peers in Jerusalem to defend his socializing with the Gentiles, I'm certain they reminded him what they'd always been taught: "Do not associate with these [Gentile] nations that remain among you" (Joshua 23:7).

Peter's response to them was revealing. He didn't debate the Scriptures with them. He didn't deny their religious tradition. He simply told them his experience, why he believed something new. He concluded by asking them, "Who was I to think that I could oppose God?" (Acts 11:17)

Peter's attitude toward Gentiles was not altered by reasonable arguments. It wasn't changed by his study of the Scripture. It wasn't even transformed by three years with Jesus. Ultimately, it took a powerful experience with God for him to turn a new way. Trusting our experiences with God will always change us.

I was raised to believe homosexuals were sexual perverts and child molesters. They were the worst of sinners and doomed for hell. I accepted this belief uncritically and, since I knew no homosexuals, found that belief easy to sustain.

Actually, I did know a homosexual. I just didn't know it. Kevin was one of my close friends. We had much in common. We went to college together, shared a deep passion for God, and ultimately both entered the ministry. I thought we shared an attraction to women. Kevin dated, talked about girls, and dreamed of marriage.

You can imagine my shock when he came to me one day and confessed his fear that he was gay. Kevin was a well-loved pastor and a committed Christian, but he'd finally begun to suspect why he wasn't attracted to the sisters, daughters, and nieces his church folk kept trying to match him up with.

I assured him he wasn't gay, and we began to pray, study Scripture, read articles, and talk together. I watched Kevin struggle and change for fifteen years. He went from "fighting his thorn in the flesh" to "not acting on his sinful desires" to "accepting how God had made him" to "seeking another man to share his life with."

He was not the only one struggling and changing. My experience with Kevin didn't match the beliefs I'd been taught and accepted so easily. He wasn't a sexual pervert or a child molester. He wasn't the worst of sinners. I knew he deeply loved God and others. Even before I'd come to believe in the salvation of every person, I couldn't imagine Kevin being damned to hell for loving someone, even if that someone was another man.

One day we had lunch together. Kevin nervously announced he'd met someone. I responded, "I'm so glad." He relaxed and began to tell me about the man he'd met. As he talked I realized two things: he was in love, and he was happier than I had ever seen him. In that moment, God made it clear to me my beliefs would have to change.

Again, I wish I could tell you words appeared on the wall of that restaurant saying, "Thus saith the Lord. 'I accept my homosexual children.'" Instead, God spent fifteen years chiseling away at my stone beliefs and softening the hardened clay of my heart.

I try to be gentle when I share my new beliefs about homosexuality with those who were taught what I once believed. I realize that if I had not had a close friend who was a Christian and a homosexual I probably would never have changed my belief. Experience is a powerful teacher. Peter might never have changed his mind if he hadn't witnessed the Holy Spirit descending on the Gentiles gathered at Cornelius's house. He couldn't deny what he'd seen. Seeing Kevin experience the same grace I knew allowed me to accept what I'd once found unacceptable.

The necessity of making room for Kevin in my life is another of those experiences that led to my belief in the salvation of every person. I began to wonder who else I'd excluded from God's grace. I began to seek out those I'd been taught to suspect, and I listened to their stories. I began talking with Mormons, Pentecostals, Muslims, Catholics, Jews, and Unitarians. I sought relationships with blacks and Hispanics, with poor people and movers and shakers, with people radically different from me. I visited prisons and became friends with murderers, rapists, and child molesters. As I made room for these people in my life here on earth, I had to consider making room for them in heaven.

These experiences have convinced me that we are all children of God longing for a grace we find far too rarely. In my life, experiencing this grace was hampered by inflexible beliefs that kept me from fully accepting

God's grace and from being gracious to those around me. I spent too much time trying to determine who was "in" and who was "out." When I began to allow God to expand my boundaries, I found my narrow beliefs challenged and ultimately changed.

I had to change. To deny experience's power to change my beliefs would be to deny God the opportunity to transform me. It would mean ignoring every vision, sign, and insight God gave me. It would require pretending that all there is to know is known, that all there is to say has been said. It would be insisting the answers I'd held the longest are the right answers.

Thomas Merton, in *No Man Is an Island,* wrote, "One of the moral diseases we communicate to one another in society comes from huddling together in the pale light of an insufficient answer to a question we are afraid to ask."[1] I'd huddled under that pale light because the process of asking questions, trusting my experiences with God, making room for those different from me, and leaving behind long-held beliefs is always painful and difficult.

Unfortunately, I wasn't alone when I huddled under that pale light. Many decide to escape the pain of growth by uncritically adopting the beliefs they were taught. One of the most discouraging responses I've received to my belief in the salvation of every person has been, "Well, that sounds good, but I've believed since I was a child that some people will go to heaven and some will go to hell. Don't ask me to change my mind now."

They then proceed to quote certain Scriptures that support what they were taught as a child. I listen politely, since I was taught these same verses. I freely admit to them that my belief is contrary to certain Scriptures. Then I cite other Scriptures that have often been ignored. They frequently scratch their heads in befuddlement. Some even ask, "If the Bible says two different things, how do we know which is true?"

I'm always glad to hear that question. I ask them, "What has been your experience with God?"

I am amazed at how often people who've been members of churches since they were children can't answer that question. For some, it may be because they've not been sensitive to God's presence in their lives. For others, I suspect it's because they've never been told their experiences with God can be trusted.

Experience and Scripture

Many people are suspicious of experiences with God. The believers in Jerusalem were suspicious of Peter's experience. You may be suspicious of mine. Some argue that such experiences aren't trustworthy, that infallible

Scripture is the only safe guide in our search for truth. They forget the Bible contains the accounts of hundreds of experiences with God. Again and again, God came to individuals and spoke to them.

Though the defenders of Biblical inerrancy are adamant that God has spoken, they grow nervous when it's suggested God continues to speak. They become frightened when someone implies God might say something different from their closely guarded interpretations of Scripture. I once shared this need to protect the Bible. Now I realize that suggesting God continues to speak doesn't lessen the value of the Bible but instead reclaims one of its central tenets.

God speaks fresh words.

I believe God spoke to the men and women of the Bible. I believe God has always spoken to his children, perhaps in an audible voice, but far more often through gentle prompting, circumstance, or other people. But I don't believe we've always gotten the message straight. This is the reason God continues to speak. He doesn't ask us to rely solely on the testimony of others. He doesn't wish to be known by rumor or reputation alone. The God who spoke to Peter is equally committed to speaking to you and me.

The Bible was never intended to end the conversation, but to encourage it. God didn't fall silent with the last chapter of Revelation. He continues to reveal himself. It makes no sense to glorify the accounts of our ancestors' encounters with God while dismissing our experiences with him today.

We who are Protestants should be especially conscious of this need to listen for the voice of God. We are the descendants of people who, based on their experiences with God, challenged the Church's interpretations of Scripture and its long-held beliefs. Martin Luther, John Wesley, George Fox, and many others described such experiences. They believed they had received a clearer vision of God's character and will.

All these people respected the Bible. Indeed, it was often in reading Scripture that they began to glimpse God's new word. But they were also open to God's leading in their lives. They understood what Jesus meant when he said, "Blessed are those who *hear* the word of God and obey it" (Luke 11:28).

I treasure the Bible. I preach from it every week. In moments of sorrow, its words have brought me comfort. In times of confusion, its commands have given me guidance. It has been a lamp to my feet and a light for my path. I say this so you'll understand that I have no desire to belittle the Bible. My complaint is with how the Bible, which challenges us to listen and obey the voice of God, is used to defend inflexible belief.

I have a friend who often says, "God said it! I believe it! And that settles it!" What my friend is really saying is this: "I read somewhere in the Bible that God said it. I believe it, even if other Scriptures contradict it. I believe it, even if others understand it differently. I believe it, even if my experience calls it into question. I believe it because I was taught it as a child. And, since believing it won't cause me the pain of change, that settles it!"

Jesus must have been responding to one of my friend's ancestors when he preached, "You have heard it said, 'An eye for an eye, a tooth for a tooth ...'" (Matthew 5:38).

Where had they heard that said? In the Bible, when the Lord said to Moses, "If anyone injures his neighbor, whatever he has done must be done to him: fracture for fracture, eye for eye, tooth for tooth" (Leviticus 24:19–20). God said it, they believed it, and that settled it for everyone but Jesus. Countering God's very words, Jesus said, "But I tell you ... if someone strikes you on the right cheek, turn to him the other also."

Jesus challenged slavish devotion to the written word. He encouraged his followers to be in relationship with a God who spoke to them personally. He invited them to step out of the rigid restraint of the letter of the law in order to experience the liberating power of grace. This has never been a popular message. Those who

claim a fresh word from God are nearly always persecuted and often killed. We embrace their words and
build them memorials only after we've buried them.

We can't have it both ways. We can't honor the
words of the men and women of the Bible while ignoring their example. They trusted their experiences with
God more than the words of those who preceded them.
They believed in a God of fresh words. How can we can-
onize their words but ignore their radical obedience to
the voice of a living God? We have become people who
read well but listen poorly.

Yet, if we were to read Scripture carefully, we would
discover an interesting truth. Of the nearly four hundred
and fifty times when Scripture speaks of the "word of
God," only a handful of references imply any written
document. In Scripture, the "word of God" is almost always spoken or heard. The word of God is a voice. It is
experienced.

Time and again, those who opposed Jesus would
quote Scripture. They would remind him of the Sabbath
law, the requirement to fast, the provision for divorce,
and the penalty for adultery. Jesus seemed unimpressed
with a person's ability to quote Scripture. His interest was
in a person's ability to hear God's voice. He said, "He who
belongs to God hears what God says" (John 8:47). To limit
the word of God to the written word is to muzzle God.

This doesn't mean I reject or ignore the Bible. It means I remember that the God I am reading about is looking over my shoulder, whispering in my ear. I've had many moments when while reading Scripture I was overwhelmed by God's presence. However, even in those moments my language was revealing. I said, "God spoke to me through this Scripture." It wasn't the Scripture speaking. It was God. Scripture will always be one powerful means by which I experience God.

Indeed, one of my first inklings that God will save every person came as I was reading the second chapter of Philippians. I had read that passage many times, but that day I experienced the words in a deeper way. Paul wrote, "God has highly exalted him and bestowed on him the name which is above every name, that at the name of Jesus *every knee should bow, in heaven and on earth and under earth, and every tongue confess that Jesus Christ is Lord, to the glory of God the Father*" (Philippians 2:9–11). In that moment, I heard the voice of God say, "Every knee and every tongue," and my eyes were opened to a possibility I'd never considered.

My first response was, "No, Lord. You can't mean every knee and every tongue." Like Peter, I would need many other visions and confirmations to overcome my reluctance. Ultimately, I would be forced to choose between trusting my experiences with God and changing my beliefs, or clinging to Scripture and tradition and ignoring God's voice. I had to decide where to pledge my allegiance.

I used to believe the Bible was the ultimate source of authority. In so doing, I elevated Scripture to a status equal with God. It eventually occurred to me that my ultimate allegiance belonged, not to the Bible, but to the One of whom it testified. When I lifted up the Bible as my ultimate authority, I made my leather-bound, gold-engraved Bible into a paper calf.

We are not to worship the Bible; we are to worship the One the Bible reveals. Too often, we clutch desperately to our Bibles, memorizing only those verses that support our views and panicking when anyone suggests God might speak a fresh word. We belong to a long tradition of people who've found it safer to trust the Scripture we can control than the God we cannot.

Jesus spoke of our reluctance to encounter God when he said, "You diligently study the Scriptures because you think that by them you possess eternal life. These are the Scriptures that testify about me, yet you refuse to come to me to have life" (John 5:39–40). Jesus invited us to look up from the page and into God's face.

Jesus never promised a written document to his followers. He promised something far more wonderful. He said, "The Holy Spirit, whom the Father will send in my name, he will teach you all things. . ." (John 14:26). To deny the Spirit's authority is to deny the very means God chose to speak to his people.

Paul understood this. He wrote, "You show that you are a letter from Christ, the result of our ministry, written not with ink but with the Spirit of the living God, not on tablets of stone, but on tablets of human hearts. . . . He has made us competent as ministers of a new covenant—not of the letter but of the Spirit; for the letter kills but the Spirit gives life" (2 Corinthians 3: 3, 6).

The testimony of the Bible is clear. The God of Jesus, of Peter and of Paul, and of Abraham and Jacob is a living God. He calls himself "I AM," not "I WAS." Scripture isn't a brittle and crumbling letter from a God long silent. The Bible proclaims a God of visions, fresh words, and new revelations. To believe the Bible is to believe in such a God.

Like Peter, I initially said no when God asked me to abandon the comfortable rules and formulas I'd cherished so long. I resisted for the same reason Peter resisted. I was afraid to trust my experience enough to question the role of Scripture and alter my beliefs. God had to overcome the same objections and misgivings you are probably experiencing right now. Perhaps your fears are even greater than mine.

Susan was one person who expressed such fears. One Sunday after church, Susan asked if she could meet with me. I invited her to stop by my office the next day. When we met, Susan announced she would be leaving our church. Of course, no church can satisfy every person (and shouldn't try), so I thanked her for being thoughtful enough to let us know she would no longer be attending.

I asked Susan if anything had happened in our church to upset her. In her three years at our church, she'd often been anxious over a variety of matters.

"It's your preaching," she said. "I know you believe God loves everyone and that everybody will finally be saved. But that's not what I learned growing up. The God I know isn't like that. I want to find a church where the pastor believes what I believe."

Having struggled as she was struggling, I responded gently. I told her she probably wouldn't have much difficulty finding such a church but that we would miss her. Then I asked Susan to consider the possibility that God might have led her to our church because her understanding of him needed to grow.

I knew from personal experience how easily we attribute all our experiences to God's hand. This habit leaves us with an understanding of God that is not only inaccurate but also potentially harmful. Just because something bad happened to us doesn't mean God caused it to happen. Just because someone treated us ungraciously doesn't mean their actions and attitudes represented God. Many false claims are made about God. They exact a heavy toll on people who believe every utterance from the pulpit must surely be the gospel truth. Unless we understand God's character and will, we easily assume every action, even the most horrible, must be credited to God.

I've learned to hold experience to the same scrutiny as the Bible, the testimony of others, and the theology I read. Those experiences I consider reliable increase our love for God, ourselves, and others. In Susan, I saw faith diminished by fear, self-esteem lowered by shame, and compassion limited by insecurity. I also realized Susan was in my office because she wanted to be freed of those obstacles to experiencing the fullness of grace.

Susan admitted the churches she had grown up in were heavy on hell and damnation and light on grace. They claimed to be "saved by grace" but then carefully outlined a very specific set of beliefs one had to accept in order to be a Christian. They had emphasized law over love. Nearly every sermon she heard growing up had warned of God's wrath. She'd been taught to fear God rather than be awed by his grace.

I asked, "And what did you learn at home?"

She blinked away tears. "I learned love is earned and that I never did quite enough to earn it. My father was a hard man."

I am saddened by how many people are afraid of God, projecting their negative experiences with parents and the Church onto God. Often we've reinforced these false images of God. I assured Susan her Father in heaven was different from her earthly father. I could tell she wanted to believe me but still hesitated.

Susan asked me, "What if you're wrong, and I believe you and go to hell?"

I replied, "Do you really think God would damn you to hell for overestimating his love?"

Susan didn't leave our church. In the following years, she cautiously opened her heart and mind to the notion that God could speak to her and she could experience him directly. But more than that, as her awareness of God's love increased, she began to suspect God felt about everyone the way he felt about her. She began to believe something beautiful about God.

Of course, her final question reveals the deeper issue hidden in any discussion of ultimate human destiny. Who is God? Is God a gracious, loving father waiting long through the night, with the light lit and the door open, confident his most defiant child will one day come home? Or is God a harsh judge eager to pass sentence, eager to punish and destroy all who do not satisfy him?

I hope you will consider the possibility that God is gracious beyond your expectation. I hope that in reading this book you'll have an experience with God that will transform you. I hope you'll hear God's voice. I hope you'll believe the very best about God. I hope you'll not be so afraid you'll shut this book and read no further.

I assure you that since I have come to believe in the ultimate triumph of God's grace, no lightning bolt has struck me, no plague has cursed my children, and no earthquake has destroyed my home. But then, the God I've experienced never does such things.

---

1. Thomas Merton, *No Man Is an Island* (New York: Harcourt Brace Jovanovich, 1955), xiii. This book of essays is full of powerful thoughts. Merton is one of those rare people capable of thinking expansively while remaining orthodox.

Three

The Character of God

I believe *God* will save every person.

When I was in seminary, I spent most of my time talking about God. I made various claims: God is love. God is holy. God is just. One day a professor asked me, "What God are you talking about?" This seemed an odd question from a man who was supposedly an expert on God.

I said, "There's only one God."

"Are you talking about Yahweh or Allah?"

I was thoroughly confused, so he began to explain. He pointed out there are hundreds of different gods people worship and that even within Christianity there are many different images of God. He suggested it's never safe to assume when you talk about God with someone that you're both talking about the same God.

I asked, "Then what God have you been teaching me about?"

"I've taught you about the God revealed in Jesus Christ."

On that day he also taught me how important it is to give some definition to the term *God*. What God do we believe in? In the previous chapter I made several claims about God: God loves everyone. God speaks to everyone. God desires a relationship with everyone. God will save everyone. I based my convictions on my experiences with God. The obvious question is whether the God I've experienced is also the God of Abraham, Isaac, and Jacob, of Jesus and of Christianity.

Can a Christian believe God will save everyone?

Obviously, if a Christian must believe the Bible is the "infallible words of God," the answer is no. There are too many verses about judgment, hell, and the eternal punishment of the wicked to make such optimism reasonable. If you are unwilling to question the Bible, neither my experiences nor my arguments will carry much weight. I had to abandon my need to protect every word of Scripture in order to consider what I now believe to be the core message of the Bible. If you believe every statement or story about God recorded in Scripture is equally true, nothing I can say will alter your conviction that God will save some and damn the rest. But I suspect many, like me, have struggled to reconcile the often contradictory biblical images of God.

When I was growing up, there was a picture in our Sunday school room of Jesus with children of every color gathered around him. You may know that picture. I imagine it hangs in nearly every Sunday school room in America. It illustrates the song heard in endless Sunday school programs—"Jesus loves the little children, all the children of the world."

This was why I found Jesus so easy to accept as a child. He loved all the little children, all the children of the world. Even though everyone in our church was white, the picture included black, Hispanic, and Asian children as well. Our teachers reminded us often that God loved them just as much as God loved us. I believed my teachers.

You can imagine my shock when as a teenager I stumbled upon a story I'd never heard taught or preached. In the tenth chapter of Joshua, the Israelites kill every man, woman, and child in the towns of Libnah, Lachish, Eglon, Hebron, and Debir. This was dreadful enough, but what horrified me was the explanation the Bible gave for their behavior: "Joshua left no survivors. He totally destroyed all who breathed, *just as the Lord, the God of Israel, had commanded*" (Joshua 10:40).

This didn't sound like the God of Jesus. When I would question this image of God I was given various explanations. Some said God was doing these children a favor since they would have grown up in an evil culture and eventually ended up in hell. When I suggested this explanation made abortion sound like an act of grace, they replied that abortion was an abomination to God. Others explained that God ordered this massacre in order to protect the people of Israel from the evil that would have come through their intermarriage with pagans. This always sounded like a rationalization Hitler might have used for destroying the Jews. The most common response to my discomfort with this image of God was "the ways of God are mysterious." I think this reply meant the person found this image equally abhorrent but couldn't overcome the belief that all the words of the Bible are equally true.

As I began to experience the grace of God in my life, I faced a dilemma. How could I reconcile stories like those of Jesus welcoming the children with stories like those of God commanding the murder of children? I'd been taught Jesus was the Son of God without any explanation for why Jesus acted differently than God. Thankfully, in the midst of this struggle I began to learn how to weigh Scripture.

Weighing Scripture is discerning which Scriptures accurately reflect God's character. If all Scripture is equally inspired and authoritative, God is as likely to swallow us up in an earthquake or drown us in a flood as God is to forgive our sin and take us into his arms. The reported behavior of God in the Bible is erratic at best and nearly double-minded in some instances. God rescues the Jewish people from the oppression of Egypt in one chapter and a few chapters later has to be convinced by Moses not to destroy them.

Weighing Scripture allows for the possibility that some descriptions of God and his behavior are inaccurate. It is not merely counting how many Scriptures say "this" about God and how many Scriptures say "that" about God and believing whichever one receives the highest score. Weighing Scripture is what Jesus taught when he was asked, "What is the greatest commandment in the law?"

If Jesus had believed that all Scriptures were of equal worth, he would have answered, "All the commandments are equally important." Instead, he replied, "Love the Lord your God with all your heart, and with all your soul, and all your mind. This is the first and greatest commandment. And the second is like it: Love your neighbor as yourself" (Matthew 22:37–39).

Then Jesus added a pivotal footnote. He said, "All the law and the prophets hang on these two commandments" (Matthew 22:40). In other words, these two verses exalting love are as heavy as the rest of the Bible. Jesus tipped the scales irrevocably in favor of love.

Love is the core message of the Bible. Paul said, "The entire law is summed up in a single command; "Love your neighbor as yourself" (Galatians 5:14). If in our examination of every chapter and verse of Scripture we miss the primacy of love, we strain out a gnat and swallow a camel. We are not "loving God with all our mind" when we refuse to do the necessary work of weighing Scripture on the scales of grace.

The primacy of love means I can't accept Joshua's claim that God commanded the genocide of his neighbors in Canaan. A God of love doesn't murder his children. A God who has commanded me to love my neighbor doesn't demand I kill that same neighbor. It is out of character. Weighing this story on the scales of grace finds it wanting.

Weighing Scripture has allowed me to avoid the all-or-nothing approach to the Bible so prevalent in Christianity. I often hear people say, "If there is one error in the Bible, how can we trust any of it?" I no longer understand this statement. It suggests the only choices are uncritical acceptance or complete rejection. To reject the Bible completely is to miss its proclamation of God's love, but to accept it uncritically is to support some ugly notions about God. The Bible has God demanding the death of those who curse their parents, commit adultery, and practice homosexuality (Leviticus 20:9–10, 13).

I remember my dismay when early in the AIDS crisis many Christian leaders explained AIDS as a punishment from God. Some seemed to find great satisfaction, even joy, in the slow and painful death of homosexuals. One of my first funerals as a pastor was for a young man who died of AIDS. His family told no one of his death and invited no one to his brief graveside service. After the funeral, his father grieved that he had failed his son. A year later, I would officiate at his funeral after he took a gun and killed himself.

Let me be perfectly clear. I no longer want anything to do with a god who punishes homosexuals by giving them a terrible disease. I want nothing to do with a god who murders children in order to maintain racial purity. I cannot believe in a god who will eternally punish a vast majority of his children. This isn't the God of Jesus. This isn't the God I have experienced. It is certainly not a god I can worship.

You may ask, "Then why did Joshua say God commanded him to murder every man, woman, and child?"

I think Joshua didn't understand the character of God very well. I believe Abraham, Isaac, and Jacob; Moses, David, and Solomon; Isaiah, Jeremiah, and Ezekiel didn't fully comprehend the character of God.

They contributed valuable insights from their experiences with God, building on the witnesses before them and laying the framework for a fuller revelation of God's character. I believe the life, death, and resurrection of Jesus was this fuller revelation.

I believe in the God of Jesus, the God he called Father.

God the Father

Every Sunday the people in my church share their prayer concerns—a woman with breast cancer, a young man needing a job, a teenager in trouble with the law, a crippled marriage. It is a litany of woe. We pray for every need.

Prayer is a mystery to me. I have seen countless prayers answered, but I'm still not sure how prayer works. I know what it isn't. It isn't about persuading an indifferent Lord or manipulating an obstinate Master or lobbying a reluctant Ruler. Prayer is more like when my son awakens in the darkness, in the grip of a nightmare, calling out "Daddy!" confident I'll come to his side.

Jesus encouraged such intimacy. The Old Testament occasionally described God as a father, but Jesus claimed "Father" as his primary image, using this term over 170 times. He gave this image more weight than any other. He told of a father who gives good gifts to his children, who knows the number of hairs on their heads, who dresses them more splendidly than the flowers of the field and feeds them more faithfully than he feeds the birds of the air. The father Jesus spoke of wasn't a stern and distant taskmaster whipping the world into shape. He was a devoted, attentive daddy who comes running to his children in night's darkest hour.

Jesus' identification of God as Father was not a sentimental fantasy. It was the core of his theology. He believed in a Father God who loved the whole world, who sought to redeem, rescue, and reconcile his children, who was willing to go to any length to save them, and who wouldn't be satisfied until all his children were seated at his table.

When he taught his disciples to pray, he didn't demand they address God as "Lord God Almighty, Creator of Heaven and Earth." He encouraged them to begin with "Our Father." Indeed, Jesus would use the most intimate form of father, "Abba," to address God. He was calling God "Daddy."

This was one of the many things Jesus taught that got him into trouble. In a culture where it was considered blasphemy to even speak the name of God, suggesting God was "our Daddy" was considered an unacceptable intimacy. When he insisted on using the term "My Father," he was accused of being demon possessed.

Today we talk of God the Father without much hesitation or thought. We no longer appreciate what a radical act it was to call the Creator of Heaven and Earth your father. Nor have we fully understood the implications of this image of God. We adamantly defend this language while largely ignoring what it implies about God. "There is . . . one God and Father of all, who is over all and through all and in all" (Ephesians 4:6).

I've been warned the image of God as Father is not always a comforting image. Many have experienced their fathers as emotionally distant, physically and sexually abusive, harsh, and demanding. Their experiences suggest a father might murder his children and God might be such a father. It is difficult for these people to find any attraction in calling God a father. It is especially painful when some of the stories about God in the Bible remind them of these abusive fathers. Even those of us who have had positive experiences with our fathers can appreciate their discomfort. If God is a father, he must be a perfect one.

I don't know any perfect parents, but I do know the qualities we expect from good parents. We expect them to love us unconditionally, to guide us, teach us, and encourage us to be our best. We count on them to set boundaries and yet give us freedom to explore and even fail. We depend on them to pick us up when we fall and hold us when we're in pain. We want them to believe in us when everyone else doubts and to claim us even in our moments of shame. This is the kind of father I've tried to be.

While I am hardly the perfect father, being a parent has helped me glimpse the heart of God. I remember how overwhelming it was to hold my firstborn in my hands and realize this was a person I had helped create. My first minutes of fatherhood taught me more about love than years of theological study. In those first few moments, I wanted nothing more than to guard, guide, and bless my child. The years since, even with all the challenges of parenting, have not diminished this desire.

When my children were little, I would ease down the hallway to their bedrooms. I would stand over their beds listening for the welcome rhythm of their breathing. If their blankets were kicked loose, I'd pull them snug. If their room was too cold, I'd lower the window. I'd smooth their hair. Any mischief they might have caused that day was forgiven in the bliss of that moment. They were my children and I loved them.

Occasionally, I'll read a story in the newspaper of a father killing his child. Such an act is beyond my comprehension. I can't fathom any loving parent harming or rejecting their child. Please carefully consider this question: Could you destroy or abandon your child? If you could, I suppose you will find nothing disturbing about the idea of God's destroying or damning his children. But if this question offends you, I invite you to ponder seriously what this means about God. Being a father is one of the experiences that has made it impossible for me to accept the idea that God will annihilate, abandon, or eternally punish any of his children.

The Reverend Jerry Falwell was once asked what he would do if his son were gay. He replied that he'd tell him that homosexuality was wrong. Then he added, "Nothing would make me reject one of my children. I would tell him to go back to his bedroom. You live here. You are my son. My resources are yours."[1] Though I'm not a fan of Jerry Falwell's theology, his response earned my respect for him as a father.

I believe God is even more gracious than Jerry Falwell. God loves his children far more perfectly than I love mine. I know how much I love my children, so I am absolutely staggered by God's love. Jesus said, "If you then, who are evil, know how to give good gifts to your children, how much more will your Father in heaven give good gifts to those who ask him!" (Matthew 7:11)

I have friends whose son has put them through hell. The boy has done everything they've forbidden, been expelled from school repeatedly, and been arrested for a variety of crimes, including stealing their car. Most recently, he ran away.

I asked the father, "How are you dealing with this?"

He replied, "I put him in the hands of God. Maybe his Father in heaven can succeed where his father on earth has failed."

I assured him God could.

This is the God I have experienced. God loves me unconditionally, guides and teaches me, and encourages me to be my best. God sets boundaries for me and yet gives me freedom to explore and even to fail. God picks me up when I fall and holds me when I am in pain. God believes in me when no one else does. God is willing to claim me even in my moments of shame. God is a father who can succeed where all other fathers fail.

Long before I believed God would save every person, I claimed God as a loving father. It took many years for me to accept that if God is a loving father, his love will persist until every one of his children is reconciled to him. I now understand why it took so long for me to recognize this truth. I had to sort through the vast variety of images of God until I found the one that matched my experience. It finally occurred to me to trust someone I believe knew God's heart—Jesus.

Choosing to trust Jesus and to call God Father has

caused me to reexamine the Bible and my theology. I've had to reject stories like Joshua's genocide. I've had to study more closely what Jesus said about love, holiness, and justice. I'm convinced God has no commitment greater than love. Everything God does, God does because of love. The Bible doesn't say God can be loving or God is often loving or even God is usually loving. It says God is love.

God Is Love

I believe God loves everyone.

Of course, nearly everyone I know believes God is loving. The Baptist who fixes my car believes it. The Catholic who runs the hardware store in my town believes it. My next-door neighbor, who sleeps in on Sundays, believes it too. I have a friend, an atheist, who even confessed, "Well, if there is a God, he must be loving."

It hasn't always been the case that divinity and love were thought synonymous. The Greek gods were fickle, jealous, and often vindictive. They treated humans with contempt and malice. The Norse gods were violent and angry. They were pictured wielding swords and axes. The Canaanite gods were bloodthirsty. They demanded the sacrifice of firstborn children to slake their thirst.

Firstborn children everywhere are grateful that our human understanding of God has matured.

The Judeo-Christian tradition was a reaction against such horrible images of God. Judaism painted a fresh picture of God. "Hear, O Israel, the Lord our God is one Lord" (Deuteronomy 6:4). Jews rejected the notion of a variety of gods with a variety of personalities. They defined God's essential character as loving. "The Lord, the Lord, the compassionate and gracious God, slow to anger, abounding in love and faithfulness, maintaining love for thousands, and forgiving wickedness, rebellion and sin" (Exodus 34:6).

Christianity built on this Jewish foundation. Love wasn't simply *one* attribute of God; it was the *chief* attribute of God. "God is love. Whoever lives in love lives in God, and God in him" (1 John 4:16). This was a stunning revelation—the inseparability of God and love.

Of course, *love* is an abstract word. It always requires some definition. What do we mean by the love of God? Is this the distant, impersonal love of a king for his subjects? Is this the exclusive love of a husband and wife? Christianity chose to follow Jesus and described this love as both intimate and all-embracing, the love of a parent for their children.

Jesus taught this universal love. He said, "A new command I give you: Love one another. As I have loved you, so you must love one another. By this, all men will know you are my disciples, if you love one another" (John 13:34–35). This may not sound like a new command since loving your neighbor was decreed in Leviticus. What was new was how Jesus defined *neighbor* and what he meant by love.

A lawyer, looking for a loophole around love, once asked Jesus, "Who is my neighbor?" Jesus told the now-famous story of the Good Samaritan. He told of a man robbed and beaten, left beside the road to die. He described how both a priest and a Levite passed by without helping the man. Then he shocked his audience by telling of a good Samaritan who rescued the man and saw to his care. Putting the words *good* and *Samaritan* together was as galling to the Jews of that day as putting the words *homosexual* and *Christian* together is to many today. The Jewish people saw the Samaritans as idolaters, faithless to God and doomed to hell. Jesus not only suggested they were the neighbor; he insinuated they were living more graciously.

Repeatedly, Jesus told stories and acted in ways that suggested, if not demanded, the people of God accept those they had labeled as unacceptable. He called on us to abandon our quick judgments and love whomever we encountered. Love was no longer reserved for those who were like us. Jesus said, "If you love those who love you, what credit is that to you?" (Luke 6:32) He went on to command us to love our enemies. Why? "Then your reward will be great, and you will be sons of the Most High, because he is kind to the ungrateful and wicked. Be merciful, just as your Father is merciful" (Luke 6:35–36).

God loves the ungrateful and wicked.

This is the father's love. His love is not limited to his obedient and submissive children. He loves his defiant and rebellious sons and daughters as well. Even when I am ungrateful and wicked, he persists in loving me. He is convinced his mercy will draw me back into his arms.

Jesus demonstrated this all-embracing love. He healed lepers. He comforted prostitutes. He ate with tax collectors. He forgave sinners. Those whom the world despised, he befriended. He died with love on his lips— "Father, forgive them; for they know not what they do" (Luke 23:34, RSV).

He challenged his followers to love as extravagantly as he loved. He commanded us to be as merciful as God is merciful. Anything short of this love would be disobedience. If God is love, as Scripture claims and my experience with God confirms, I must reject any word that suggests God is less than loving. I must abandon any reasoning that allows me to be less gracious than God.

Perhaps I was too hard on Joshua. He grew up in a

less enlightened age when people didn't fully understand God's character. He didn't have the gracious words of Hosea or the example of Jesus. He never received a vision like Peter. He would have been afraid to boldly claim God as father. There is a reasonable explanation for Joshua's behavior. He didn't know better. But how can I excuse my years of insisting in one breath that God is love while in the next breath pronouncing God's eternal damnation of millions of his children?

There is a simple explanation for my double-minded behavior. I had a double-minded image of God. This image allowed me to justify my hateful attitudes and behaviors toward other human beings. I could proclaim God's grace in one breath and God's wrath in the next. God's character was dependent on my circumstance and mood. When I realized my own sinfulness, I claimed, "God is love, and I am forgiven." When others sinned against me, I proclaimed, "God is angry, and you're gonna be sorry."

Too often, the God of wrath was a divine pit bull to sic on my enemies. I was thankful God had loved and saved me. But I secretly delighted that God would destroy those people I disliked. Such twisted thinking made God "my Father" rather than "our Father." God was gracious to me but not to others.

I think I clung to the God of wrath so tenaciously because I can be a wrathful person. I find grace and forgiveness difficult. Judgment and condemnation come easily to me. When attacked, I retaliate. Turning the other cheek is not natural. I must choose to do that. My instinct, my first impulse, is toward wrath and revenge.

I recently read in the newspaper of the sentencing of a man convicted of manslaughter. He'd been driving drunk and slammed into another car, killing the other driver, who was a husband and father of two.

At the sentencing, he was given the maximum sentence of eight years in prison.

The victim's widow asked to speak at his hearing. She said, "You may serve only eight years in prison, but you'll spend eternity burning in hell."

Her response was perfectly understandable. It would have been unnatural for her to say, "I forgive you." For many years I would have applauded such sentiments.

Wrath came easily to me. Because it came easily to me, I assumed it came easily to God. I was reluctant to abandon the biblical images of an angry God because this is the God I would be. I preferred living with this spiritual split-mindedness, forever vacillating between a God of love and a God of wrath, rather than accepting the gracious character of God and living as a grateful, forgiving child.

Nowhere is such spiritual split-mindedness more evident than in our statements about human destiny. On the one hand, we assert God is loving and merciful. On the other hand, we believe God will forever torture the very people most in need of forgiveness. We seldom question the jarring contrasts of such beliefs, preferring to live with the inconsistencies rather than be transformed by God's grace.

Frank hadn't been to church in years. He was my neighbor, and we had befriended each other. His children came to church and participated in our youth activities. I officiated at his daughter's wedding. When his wife nearly died of emphysema, I sat with her in the hospital. Many times over those years I invited Frank to church. He'd always laugh and say, "Pastor, the ceiling would fall in if I came to church."

One Sunday, to my surprise, Frank hesitantly walked into our sanctuary and took a seat near the back. He was wearing worn blue jeans and the cleanest flannel shirt he owned. He fumbled his way through the service, usually finding the hymn about the time we finished singing it. He listened intently as I preached and nodded his head several times in agreement.

After worship, Frank came down the aisle and shook my hand, "Pastor," he said, "aren't you surprised the ceiling didn't fall in?"

I peered at the ceiling.

"It didn't fall in," I said, "but I do notice a few new cracks."

We laughed.

Of course, neither Frank's discomfort nor my response is all that funny. It is sad that so many people share Frank's unease. They don't expect to be greeted by a loving Father. They imagine a father with a belt in his hand and wrath in his eyes. They don't expect grace.

So many people enter churches persuaded God is lurking in ambush. They come expecting fire and brimstone, and we've been all too willing to heap it on. We've slandered God's character too long. I regret the times I manipulated and coerced others with sermons designed to shame and frighten rather than celebrate the love of God. I failed to appreciate the depth of God's love.

Paul said, "I pray that you, being rooted and established in love, may have the power, together with all the saints, to grasp how wide and long and high and deep is the love of Christ, and to know this love that surpasses knowledge—that you may be filled to the measure of all the fullness of God" (Ephesians 3:17–19).

I now share his prayer. The more I experience the love of God, the more I realize that this love surpasses knowledge. God's love is wide enough to include us all. It is long enough to last through eternity. It is higher than any human love we've known. It reaches into the deepest hell and redeems the lost.

The world needs to know that God's eternal, extravagant love is not *part* of the gospel. It is the *whole* gospel.

Those who are ungrateful and wicked need to know God loves them. They are not objects of God's wrath. Their reconciliation is the desire of God's heart. They need to know the ceiling will never fall. It is held up by grace.

God Is Holy

I know a woman who is fanatically clean. Her home is spotless. She dons white gloves and moves from room to room, checking for dust. The furniture in her house is covered in plastic.

I went to visit her once. She invited me into her front room, apologizing for how filthy her house was. I sat on the couch's cold plastic, and we chatted. She offered me some iced tea and placed my glass on a coaster on the coffee table. After a sip, I inadvertently placed the glass on the wood of the coffee table. She glared at the glass, suddenly oblivious to everything else, until I realized my mistake.

When I left, I suspect she washed down the couch with disinfectant, sprayed air freshener through the room, polished the coffee table, and washed my glass in boiling water. She was obsessed.

Sometimes we talk as if God is similarly obsessed.

Often when I speak about the love of God, someone will point out all the verses in which God is called holy. They suggest there are competing commitments within God. God is loving, but God is also holy. God desires the salvation of every person, but God also demands those in relationship to him be perfect as he is perfect.

Holiness has usually been understood as moral perfection or purity. God has been pictured in a sparkling white robe, sitting on a heavenly throne high above human contamination. God desires relationship with us but grows squeamish at the very thought of touching or being touched by such disgusting creatures. This theology asserts that our sinfulness makes it impossible for God to relate with us.

One of the ugliest ideas I've heard about God involves his attitude while Jesus was on the cross. I've often heard preachers say the reason it became dark at the moment of Christ's death was because God, in his holiness, could not look upon sin. Jesus was bearing the sins of the world. Therefore, God turned his back on him.

The idea that clouds could somehow shield God from seeing what was happening is silly enough. Far more dangerous is the belief that God will not tolerate, relate to, look upon, or care for those who are sinners. Jesus seemed to think that sinners were precisely who God was most interested in. He told the Pharisees, "It is not the healthy who need a doctor, but the sick. I have not come to call the righteous, but sinners" (Mark 2:17). Of course, this is what irritated so many about Jesus. He believed God was more interested in people than in purity.

What would the Bible be like if God valued purity more than people? Consider how a well-known story might have ended:

> The scribes and Pharisees brought to Jesus a woman who had been caught in adultery. Throwing her at his feet, they said to Jesus, "Teacher, this woman has been caught in the act of adultery. In the law Moses commanded us to stone such a woman. What do you say?"
>
> Jesus said to them, "The law is clear. We'll have to kill her."
>
> And saying that, he picked up a rock and threw it at her, striking her on the head.
>
> The scribes and Pharisees joined in with great enthusiasm, throwing stones at the woman until she was dead.
>
> Then Jesus turned to them and said, "Let she who is with sin be stoned."
>
> And the scribes and Pharisees marveled at his devotion to purity.

Thankfully, this isn't what happened.

Instead, Jesus pointed out the sinfulness of all people and forgave the women. It was acts of grace such as this that led to his arrest and murder. Grace is a scandal when we're infatuated with moral purity.

Jesus rejected our obsession with moral purity. Jesus believed he wasn't made spiritually impure by touching sinful men and women. Indeed, he was convinced just the opposite was true. Sinful men and women were made clean by his touch.

Jesus once encountered a leper. Lepers were considered unclean, and to touch them was to be made impure.

> The leper knelt before Jesus and said, "Lord, if you are willing, you can make me clean." Jesus reached out his hand and touched the man. "I am willing," he said. "Be clean." (Matthew 8:2–3)

Like the leper, I used to approach God hesitantly, keenly aware of my deformities and imperfections, afraid of rejection. I knelt before God unsure of God's willingness to touch me and love me and call me his own. The good news is that *God is willing*.

When my son was five we were preparing to attend some function where we all needed to be well dressed. We gave my son a bath and put on his nicest clothes, and then my wife and I began to prepare ourselves. Our son, bored and impatient, asked to go outside and play. We finally gave in but made it clear he was not to get dirty. He promised to be good.

About five minutes after he went outside, our doorbell rang. I went to the door. Standing at our doorstep was our neighbor and a little boy with mud caked from the very top of his head to the tip of his toe. He had tried to jump over a mud puddle and failed. Our neighbor asked, "Is this your son?"

For a moment I thought about saying no. But grace won out. I took him by the hand and led him upstairs to his second bath. I claimed him and I cleaned him. His filthy condition did not change our relationship. Indeed, it only emphasized how much he needed me.

My experience with God and my examination of Scripture have convinced me that God delights in getting his hands dirty, lifting men and women from the gutter and cleansing them. True holiness delights in restoring the impure.

What then does it mean to say God is holy?

Holiness is God's ability to confront evil without being defiled. God's holiness does not require him to keep evil at arm's length. God's holiness enables him to take the wicked in his arms and transform them. God is never in danger of being defiled. No evil can alter his love, for his gracious character is beyond corruption. This is what it means to say God is holy—God's love is incorruptible.

Holiness and love are not competing commitments. God is love. His love endures forever. This enduring love is what makes God holy. No manner of evil done to us or by us can separate us from this love. God transforms his morally imperfect children through the power of his perfect love. It is our experience of this love that inspires us to such perfection.

Jesus said, "Be perfect, therefore, as your heavenly father is perfect" (Matthew 5:48). If this verse was a command for moral perfection, our cause is hopeless. Fortunately, this admonition follows a command to "love your enemies and pray for those who persecute you" (Matthew 5:44). Perfection is demonstrated not by moral purity, but by extravagant love. We are like God not when we are pure, but when we are loving and gracious.

Hosea, perhaps one of the most gracious writers of the Hebrew Scriptures, tells of God's decision to love his ungrateful, wicked children. The eleventh chapter contrasts God's persistent love and care with Israel's continual sin and rebellion. At that point, where most Hebrew texts would announce God's judgment and destruction, Hosea voices a different response.

God says, "How can I give you up, Ephraim? How can I hand you over, Israel? How can I treat you like Admah? How can I make you like Zeboiim? My heart is changed within me; all my compassion is aroused. I will not carry out my fierce anger, nor will I turn and devastate Ephraim. For I am God, and not man—the Holy one among you. I will not come in wrath." (Hosea 11:8–9)

The Holy One will never come in wrath.
The Holy One always comes in love.

God Is Just

Whenever I speak of the salvation of every person, someone objects that such an expansive grace is unjust. God is loving, but he is also just. They mention Hitler, Stalin, or the latest serial killer and argue that extravagant grace is a denial of justice. Justice and grace become competing commitments with grace always coming in second. I sympathize with this sentiment. It used to be mine.

Growing up, I spent nearly every Saturday afternoon at the Royal Theater. I'd do my chores in the morning, and my parents would give me fifty cents to go to the movies. My favorites were the Westerns. I remember watching the movie *Shane* starring Alan Ladd. It was the story of a retired gunfighter who takes a job as a farmhand, only to have the evil rancher, Ryker, abuse the townsfolk.

By the end of the movie, I'd worked myself into a bloodlust and was elated when Shane reluctantly strapped on his pistols and blasted the bad guys in a hail of lead. Shane may have been reluctant, but I was overjoyed. I wasn't alone. The theater was full of skinny, nerdy boys who'd suffered at the hands of bullies but lacked the courage to do anything about it. Shane's triumph was ours, and we stood and cheered.

The next day, Sunday, I went to church and heard stories about a meek and mild Jesus teaching about love, healing the sick, and feeding the hungry. But one day, his mercy strained to the limit, he reluctantly took up a whip, went to the Temple, and turned over the tables of those who abused the poor. I always liked that story. In my imagination, Jesus looked remarkably like Alan Ladd.

Then the story took a twist. Jesus was arrested, convicted on trumped-up charges, flogged, and nailed to a cross. His followers scattered while his enemies celebrated his demise. Still, I'd watched enough Westerns to know never to give up on the hero. The train might be bearing down, the fuse on the gunpowder keg lit, his fate apparently sealed, but I never despaired.

So Jesus' resurrection didn't surprise me. Heroes never die. They return to destroy their enemies. If the disciples had been raised on Saturday matinees, they would have waited at the tomb, confident of Jesus' triumph.

It was what happened after the resurrection that disappointed me. Jesus didn't follow the script. He should have returned to the Temple and blasted his enemies. He should have marched into the Roman palace to find Pilate quaking in fear, begging for mercy. All of Jerusalem should have carried Jesus on their shoulders and proclaimed him king. That's how Hollywood would have ended the Easter story.

Jesus would never have made it in Hollywood. Instead of vanquishing his enemies and parading in triumph, Jesus met with his friends and encouraged them. Not a single verse indicates Jesus made his resurrection known to his enemies. Neither did he urge his disciples to avenge his suffering. He told them to preach, teach, and heal—to spread his gospel of love. Instead of using the resurrection as evidence of his power, he used it to serve, cooking breakfast for his followers. Instead of using the resurrection as an opportunity to wreak revenge, he used it to offer forgiveness, pardoning Peter for his betrayal. It is an odd ending.

The book of Revelation, with its promise of justice, offered the ending I sought. Jesus returns on a white horse, a bloody sword in hand. He leads an army, defeats his enemies, and casts them into hell. That kind of finale sells tickets. Movies that end with the hero cooking breakfast for his friends, teaching love and forgiveness, don't fill theaters.

My hunger for justice was another obstacle to my embracing God's universal grace. I wish I could blame my thirst for revenge on Hollywood, but Hollywood didn't create it. The movies simply satisfied my craving for unsparing justice. Such justice had only one concern—balancing the scales. Forgetting that Christianity's symbol is a cross, I believed God stood blindfolded, weighing our deeds, demanding pain be answered with pain, injury with injury, until the heavenly scales drew level. I confused God with Lady Justice.

I applauded "life for life, eye for eye, tooth for tooth, hand for hand, foot for foot, burn for burn, wound for wound, bruise for bruise" (Exodus 21:23–25). This code of justice was clear and fair. You received exactly what you deserved. It was also cold and heartless. Though it slowed the escalating cycle of violence common to humanity, it still returned pain for pain, injury for injury. It left no room for grace and was incapable of bringing healing. As Tevye in *Fiddler on the Roof* said, "An eye for eye and a tooth for tooth just leaves the world blind and toothless."

The more I experienced God's grace, the less retributive justice appealed. Yet I was reluctant to forgive those who'd hurt me. For many years, I spoke out of both sides of my mouth. I expected grace for myself and those I loved but insisted on justice for my enemies. Patiently and tenderly, God convinced me of mercy's triumph over judgment.

Now I believe God has never been blind to our pain and brokenness and is always moved to heal us. Wielding a sword, especially while blindfolded, only causes new wounds. Such justice is powerless to end pain, heal injury, reconcile enemies, and restore God's children to relationship. Since God desires a world free of mourning, crying, or pain, the old order of "eye for an eye and tooth for a tooth" must pass away.

We bristle at this, unwilling to abandon our obsession with balancing a heavenly ledger. We resist the command of Jesus to abandon our infatuation with justice. He said, "You have heard that it was said, 'Eye for eye and tooth for tooth.' But I tell you, do not resist an evil person. If someone strikes you on the check, turn to him the other also" (Matthew 5:38–39). Obeying this command requires us to lay aside the scales of justice, close our ledgers, hammer our spears into plows, and, like Jesus, willingly absorb the pain of the world.

To turn the other cheek is to choose grace over justice. It is to trust the redemptive power in this choice. It is to invite the one who causes pain to repent and be restored to relationship. It is to absorb pain rather than inflict it.

In choosing grace over wrath, God laid the foundation of his kingdom upon forgiveness and reconciliation, not upon revenge or even justice. Grace is the bedrock of the kingdom. Those who aspire to this kingdom must choose between their love of justice and their need for grace. Unjustly condemned, Jesus could have demanded "a life for a life." Instead, he prayed, "Father, forgive them; they know not what they do" (Luke 23:34, KJV). Grace, not justice, was his choice. After his resurrection, having already forgiven his enemies, he saw no need to destroy them.

In so doing, Jesus taught his followers this alternative to justice. "I tell you who hear me: Love your enemies, do good to those who hate you, bless those who curse you, pray for those who mistreat you" (Luke 6:27–28). Rather than measuring the pain others afflict and paying them back a carefully calibrated equal amount, we are to overflow with love, goodness, blessing, and prayer. These acts of grace achieve what justice cannot—God's new heaven and new earth.

I no longer believe Christ will return in vengeance and God will cast many in hell for all eternity. Such a future contradicts the example of Jesus and the character of God. I understand the need for punishment and consequence. Since I punish my children for their misbehaviors, I can hardly deny God's right to correct his. My trouble is with eternal punishment. No loving parent would send their child to their room forever.

People often offer the story of the rich man and Lazarus in the sixteenth chapter of Luke as evidence of God's justice and eternal punishment. In that story, Jesus tells of a rich man living the good life while a beggar named Lazarus starves at his gate. In the next life, Lazarus is in paradise while the rich man languishes in hell. The story ends with Abraham and Lazarus refusing to dip their fingers in water to relieve the rich man's agony. The only act of compassion is the rich man's request that someone warn his five brothers.

Where is the justice in this story? Even when judged by the command of an "eye for an eye, and a tooth for a tooth," the rich man's sentence seems excessive. How do we justify punishing a lifetime of sin with an eternity of suffering? At what point are the scales balanced?

I can accept that repentance and transformation may require some to experience the misery they caused. When my son was a toddler and began biting everyone he met, my wife finally resorted to biting him. Experiencing that pain cured him of his behavior. Perhaps

Hitler will repent only after experiencing some of the agony he wrought. Or perhaps he'll discover what I've discovered—the deepest pain is the inward awareness of the hurt I've caused others. Regardless, I am unable to see how the eternal punishment of anyone could bring glory to God.

Love and punishment are not mutually exclusive. But parental punishment is never designed to inflict pain. It desires to redeem, shape, or protect. When it is excessive, it becomes abuse. Eternal punishment contradicts even the harshest concepts of justice. It defies God's commitment to restoring all things.

Fortunately, a violent and vengeful final judgment is not the only biblical image of our ultimate destiny. Paul writes, "He [God] has made known to us the mystery of his will according to his good pleasure, which he purposed in Christ, to put into effect when the times will have reached their fullness—to bring *all* things in heaven and on earth together under one head, even Christ" (Ephesians 1:9–10).

Thomas Talbott, in his wonderful book, *The Inescapable Love of God,* notes that some early church fathers, namely Origen and St. Jerome, took this verse so seriously they believed God would ultimately be reconciled with Satan.[2] Some are appalled by such far-reaching forgiveness. They insist damnation is evidence of God's justice.

I believe, as with holiness, we've misunderstood justice. Justice is the end rather than the means. It is the result of God's gracious kingdom, not the tool to bring it about. It is making all things just as they were intended to be. Working for justice means eliminating the causes of pain, not increasing them. In feeding the hungry, healing the sick, encouraging the oppressed, and challenging the oppressor, Jesus asked us to sow goodness, not multiply misery.

We are called to be ambassadors of reconciliation, modeling God's passion for seeing animosity ended and injury forgiven. Justice may equalize rights and pains, but only grace can transform hearts. Dr. Martin Luther King Jr. was not satisfied with forcing white Americans to give black Americans their rights. He sought more than retribution. In *Strength to Love* he wrote,

> We shall match your capacity to inflict suffering by our capacity to endure suffering. We shall meet your physical force with soul force. Do to us what you will, and we shall continue to love you. Throw us in jail, and we shall still love you. Bomb our homes and threaten our children, and we shall still love you. Send your hooded perpetrators of violence into our community at the midnight hour and beat us and leave us half

dead, and we shall still love you. But be assured that we will wear you down by our capacity to suffer. One day we shall win freedom, but not only for ourselves. We shall so appeal to your heart and conscience that we shall win *you* in the process, and our victory will be a double victory.[3]

Only love has the power to bring a double victory. Retribution and revenge are incapable of giving us the reconciliation we deeply desire. Coercion, punishment, and wrath are incapable of creating the kingdom of God. They represent the weakest form of power. They are an admission of a failure to persuade and attract. They respond to resistance with violence and destruction. Yet to destroy or eternally punish another is evidence only of our inability to transform them. To choose grace is to reject those means powerless to bring reconciliation.

A friend tells a story of a day when his two young sons were driving him crazy—bickering and fighting and tattling on each other. Finally, his younger son, Michael, came complaining that his older brother, Daniel, had hit him.

My friend, fed up with it all, called Daniel into the room. He told Michael he had permission to hit Daniel. Michael, remembering all the times his parents had said, "We don't hit," hesitated. So my friend said, "Hit him back, Michael." So Michael hit Daniel. Daniel began to cry. Then, to my friend's surprise, Michael began to cry too.

My friend told me later, "I suddenly realized I'd failed my boys. Michael had come seeking my help in healing the breach between his brother and him. He wanted them to be able to play together peacefully. He wanted reconciliation, and all I gave him was revenge."

I once counseled a woman who'd been molested by her father. Initially, we focused on the pain her father had caused and how badly she wanted him to experience that same pain. Over time, our conversations changed. She realized she didn't want her father to be punished. She simply wanted him to say, "I'm sorry. Please forgive me." Eventually, she admitted her deepest desire: "What I really want is for my father to love me as a father should." She discovered her deepest hunger wasn't for revenge but for reconciliation.

Retribution documents every hurt and injury, but "love keeps no record of wrongs" (1 Corinthians 13:5). It took many years for me to fully appreciate this verse. It is an utter denial of the idea that God is a cosmic moral bookkeeper scrutinizing our every word and examining our every action. God is not keeping track of our sins in order to determine the very moment our sins exceed his forgiveness. God keeps no record of wrongs because God knows his unfailing love will ultimately make all wrongs right. Only when we too cease keeping our careful accounts of pains owed and injuries unpaid can we discover the freedom to forgive and the possibility of reconciliation.

I grew up imagining the Judgment as that moment when God reviewed our lives and pointed out every hidden and shameful act. Now I imagine a much different scene. God will not dwell on our wrongs. They will be unrecorded, forgiven and forgotten. God will not sit on a throne with the scales of justice in his hand. God will run to embrace even his most wayward child. All will be healed. All will be forgiven. All will be reconciled.

This may not seem like good news to you. It wasn't always to me. It wasn't to John the Baptist. Known for his fire-and-brimstone preaching, he said, "The ax is already at the root of the trees, and every tree that does not produce good fruit will be cut down and thrown in the fire" (Matthew 3:10). He spoke of Jesus as the one who would "clear his threshing floor, gathering the wheat into the barn and burning up the chaff with unquenchable fire" (Matthew 3:12).

Jesus must have been a grave disappointment to him. Jesus spoke of love, forgiveness, and grace. John became so disillusioned he sent some of his disciples to question Jesus. They asked, "Are you the one who was to come, or should we expect someone else?" (Luke 7:20)

Jesus answered, "Go back and report to John what you have seen and heard. The blind receive sight, the lame walk, those who have leprosy are cured, the deaf hear, the dead are raised, and the good news is preached to the poor. Blessed is the man who does not fall away on account of me" (Luke 7:22–23).

Jesus offered reconciliation and healing, rather than judgment and retribution, as evidence of his divine mandate. He refused to be the man John desired or expected. He understood how difficult it would be for John, and for us, to accept his message of grace. He knew forgiveness would be perceived as a miscarriage of justice. He also knew only grace can bring about God's will—the restoration of all things.

God's response to evil isn't a clenched fist. God doesn't repay evil with evil. God is convinced his unyielding grace will wear evil down to nothing. The more I experience God's grace, the more I am persuaded of its power to restore even the most wicked to relationship with God and one another. For what good is grace—this unconditional love of God—if it is not extended to those who deserve it the least but need it the most?

God is love. Holiness and justice are not competing commitments. God has not chosen to turn his back on us or to punish us as our sins deserve. God has chosen to redeem us. Nothing requires God to condemn us, so God has not. Rather, in his sovereign freedom, he waits patiently for the day of our redemption.

When I was a child, I sat in a darkened theater, reveling in retribution. Those days are gone. Now I long for a day when the lion lies down with the lamb, the cow feeds with the bear, and the child plays in the viper's nest. In this peaceable kingdom, "they will neither harm nor destroy on all God's holy mountain, for the earth will be full of the knowledge of the Lord, as the waters cover the sea" (Isaiah 11:9).

My hope is God's promise.

1. "Tensions and Snubs, Some Conciliation as Falwell, Gays Meet," *USA Today,* October 25, 1999.

2. Thomas Talbott, *The Inescapable Love of God* (Parkland, FL: Universal Publishers, 1999), 15. This is a wonderful apologetic for Christian universalism. Talbott argues that Roman imperial politics ended a healthy debate in early Christianity concerning human destiny. He also offers an extensive exegesis of both universalist and dualistic references in the New Testament.

3. Martin Luther King Jr., *Strength to Love* (Philadelphia: Fortress Press, 1963), 56. This quote comes from a sermon titled "Loving Your Enemies." Both Gandhi and King based their call for nonviolence on the conviction that love always and ultimately overcomes evil.

Four

The Will of God

I believe God *will* save every person.

I remember the first time I heard those words. I was talking with a good friend, and we were decrying some act of evil. I said, "Even hell is too good for some people."

My friend cringed when I spoke those words. He hesitated and then said softly, "I don't believe in hell. I believe God will save every person."

I was shocked. My friend was a faithful Christian and a thoughtful person. We'd spoken often of God, the Church, and the world with little disagreement. I'd never suspected him of such heresy.

I said, "How can you believe that?"

He replied, "How can you believe that God's grace isn't sufficient, that many of God's children will languish in hell forever, that they'll never be restored to their Father, that evil will claim victory in so many lives? How can you believe that?"

His questions were as valid as mine. While it would be many years before I spoke at Sally's funeral and shared my friend's confidence in God's grace, his questions forced me to examine my assumptions about human destiny. How could I believe many were destined for eternal punishment?

My initial answer was that the Bible repeatedly warned of the punishment of the wicked, the final judgment, and the fires of hell. Such predictions weren't limited to the book of Revelation. Jesus said, "Enter through the narrow gate. For wide is the gate and broad the road that leads to destruction, and many enter through it. But small is the gate and narrow the road that leads to life, and only a few find it" (Matthew 7:13–14). Two roads and two destinies have been a common theme of Jewish and Christian theology.

My friend acknowledged that believing God would save all his children was a less-traveled path, but he disputed my claim that universal salvation was a New Age phenomenon. He told me of Origen and Gregory of Nyssa—early church fathers who believed in the salvation of all people. He spoke of champions of God's grace, seldom tolerated and often silenced, in other generations.

He pointed out the Scriptures that led these saints to consider a different ending to the human story. He challenged me to ask the question they wrestled with: "Why must some be damned?" Could I give an answer other than "the Bible says so"?

My search revealed two common justifications for the salvation of some and damnation of many. The first suggested *God doesn't want to save all his children.* God could but chooses not to. God has favorites and saves only those who please him. The second admitted God wants to save all his children but reluctantly concluded *God can't save all his children.* God can't but wishes he could. God respects our freedom to reject his grace and doom ourselves to damnation.

Both explanations have problems. The first defends the power of God while diminishing God's affection. The second affirms God's love but reduces its power and reach. Both positions assume some will be damned. The first concludes this is God's will, that his judgment is beyond reproach even if it includes the eternal torment of his children. The second implies God's will is irrelevant, that we are the ones who control our destiny and determine God's attitude toward us. Neither view takes seriously the possibility that God loves and saves every person.

I too tried to ignore that possibility. Convinced the accounts of God's wrath must be true, I initially defended both grace and judgment. Even though I'd experienced the persistence of God's grace, I adopted elaborate schemes for why some would resist God's love and be damned. Even as God's love was transforming my life, I doubted its power in other lives. Although I insisted grace was a divine gift, I thought it a temporary dispensation. God's love did not endure forever.

I took comfort, even pleasure, in believing those who did great evil would someday pay a horrible price. I knew vengeance belonged to the Lord, but I hoped to be a spectator when the wicked got their due. Anyone who has been a victim of evil has likely shared my fantasy.

I once met a man who personified evil. Tony was self-centered, verbally and physically abusive to his family, lazy, and alcoholic. When I challenged his behavior, he forbade his family to attend church. When I continued to send his wife and children birthday cards, he threatened my life.

I wish I could say I prayed for the one who persecuted me, but my initial response wasn't so noble. When I heard Tony was seriously ill, I found myself hoping for his death. I thought his death would be a blessing to his family and an act of divine justice. Then I read, "As surely as I live, declares the Sovereign Lord, I take no pleasure in the death of the wicked, but rather that they turn from their ways and live" (Ezekiel 33:11). I realized I didn't share God's desire.

I began to pray for Tony's transformation. I imagined how his redemption would bless his wife and family. I thought about the beauty of such a man repenting. My hate for Tony decreased as my hope for him increased. While Tony has not yet yielded to grace, my struggle to love him changed me.

I learned God is never glorified by wrath. God's power is never demonstrated in his capacity to punish but rather is shown in his ability to transform and redeem the wicked—those who do evil and those who hope for the death of evildoers. Wrath is always evidence of the absence of grace. Choosing wrath is choosing evil. It means destroying our enemies rather than loving them.

Eventually, my arguments for God's wrath rang hollow. My experiences with God made them unbelievable. God responded to my disobedience with gentle and gracious guidance rather than destruction. My study of Jesus' life and words convinced me grace was the heart of his message. He came not to condemn the world but to proclaim God's salvation. My experiences as a pastor persuaded me of grace's power to save and transform. They also exposed the ugliness of graceless religion. Those in my congregations most obsessed with holiness and justice were the least attractive Christians. I found myself hoping God wasn't like them. Eventually, I too chose the less-traveled path.

I believe God wants to, can, and will save every person.

God desired Tony's salvation long before I did. From the moment he was formed, God loved him. His redemption was God's constant desire, and what God desired, he could accomplish. Not Tony's troubled mind, not his destructive lifestyle or his hostility toward the Church, not even his selfishness changed God's heart toward him. Because God had determined to save him, not even he could ultimately separate himself from God's love.

My confidence in God's desire to redeem Tony convinced me of God's will for the world. Salvation is not a matter of good works or right doctrine. Salvation is an act of God, born of his desire, ability, and determination to redeem us. "He saved us not because of the righteous things we had done, but because of his mercy" (Titus 3:5).

The Desire of God

I once took a group of twenty-five teenagers to Chicago. We visited the lakeshore, the zoo, the museums, and a shopping mall. At each stop, I carefully counted how many children were on the bus before we left for our next destination. When we arrived at our final stop of the day, a famous downtown pizzeria, we discovered one of our girls was missing.

I panicked. I took no comfort in the fact that at every previous stop we had accounted for every child. I didn't celebrate that we had twenty-four of the twenty-five— 96 percent of the children we began with, an A in any classroom in America. I knew my commitment to the parents of those children required 100 percent. I rushed back to the shopping mall to find our lost girl. Fortunately, she was waiting patiently at the front door of the mall, certain we'd return for her.

My experience reminded me of a story of Jesus. He told of a man who owned a hundred sheep and had one wander off. The man left the ninety-nine and went in search of his lost lamb. Jesus concluded, "In the same way your Father in heaven is not willing that any of his little ones should be lost" (Matthew 18:14). Like any good father, when it comes to his children's welfare, God isn't satisfied with anything less than 100 percent.

This shouldn't have surprised me. I'd always admired God's heart. I never doubted God's interest in saving every person. Paul, when encouraging the Church to pray for everyone, said, "This is good and pleases God our Savior, who wants *all* men to be saved and to come to a knowledge of the truth" (1 Timothy 2:3–4). I was convinced of God's passion toward the despised, desperate, and depraved. This conviction inspired my first visits to nursing homes, homeless shelters, and prisons. I worked for the salvation of all even when I thought it impossible.

One of my first sermons was at an inner city mission. I watched about fifty men, many mentally ill or drunk, herded into a dingy chapel. They mumbled the words to a familiar hymn, yawned through the prayers, and seemed oblivious to the words I'd labored over so carefully. I pleaded with them to accept Christ and experience his grace. No one responded. Afterward, I turned to one of the workers and said, "Well, that was hopeless."

He smiled and said, "I used to be one of them."

This was the first of many experiences that dispelled my pessimism. As I studied the Bible, I discovered it full of once-hopeless men and women redeemed by God. As a pastor, I encountered people whose stories spoke of God's ability to lift the most miserable from the muck. I became convinced no one was beyond God's reach. God longed to save us all.

I was appalled the first time I encountered the doctrine of predestination. Predestination asserts God has predetermined who will be saved and who will be damned. Though many Christians have been uncomfortable with this diminishing of divine love and human freedom, this theology does offer one explanation for the damnation of many: God doesn't want to save everyone.

Before rejecting this idea outright, we need to recognize its support in Scripture. God's arbitrary decision to choose Israel and reject other nations was a recurring theme of the Hebrew Scriptures. This concept of divine sovereignty was less prominent in the early church but still present. Paul wrote, "What if God, choosing to show his wrath and make his power known, bore with great patience the objects of his wrath prepared for destruction? What if he did this to make the riches of his glory known to the objects of his mercy, whom he prepared in advance for glory?" (Romans 9:22–23) Such thinking led Paul, Augustine, Calvin, and many others to suggest some were elected for salvation and others for damnation.

The elect were those predestined by God for mercy. They were God's favorites, his chosen, his adopted children. The remainder were the wicked, the pagans, the children of the evil one. God was not the father of all but the father of the elect, which invariably included only those who held this theology.

This limiting of God's affection persists. John MacArthur, a popular Christian leader, wrote a book titled *The God Who Loves: He Will Do Whatever It Takes to Draw Us to Him.* Though it has a wonderful title, the book argues for a God of limited love. MacArthur writes,

> No one ought to conclude that because God's love
> is universally extended to all that God therefore

loves everyone equally. The fact that God loves every man and woman does not mean that He loves all alike. Clearly he does not.[1]

MacArthur argues for the election of some to salvation and many to damnation. He implies God hates some of his children. He writes, "God loves the world, but He loves 'His own' perfectly, unchangingly, completely, fully, comprehensively."[2] Which is to say that God loves others imperfectly. According to MacArthur, God's unconditional love has one major condition: it is only for a select few.

This is a stunning denial of God's universal love. It makes God's love limited and arbitrary. It diminishes God's grace in order to sustain God's wrath. It emphasizes God's freedom to destroy the work of his hands while dismissing God's freedom to have mercy on whom he will have mercy. It gives lip service to God's universal love but is mysteriously silent about how damnation is an act of love. Indeed, its proponents often dodge such difficult questions with the response, "It's a mystery."

Though I never found predestination compelling, I understand its motivation. It tries to defend every biblical claim about God. If Scripture says God sent two bears to kill forty-two youths for calling the prophet Elisha "Baldy," it must be true. If Scripture says God will cast many of his children into hell, he must have a good reason. This defense of biblical inerrancy makes distinctions between good and evil irrelevant. If God did it, it must be good. Unfortunately, this interpretation of God's past activity has dangerous ramifications for the present.

Every event becomes an act of God. If your child dies of crib death, it's God's will. If your home is destroyed by a tornado, that too is part of God's predetermined plan. The objects of God's wrath have no right to complain. "Does not the potter have the right to make out of the same lump of clay some pottery for noble purposes and some for common use?" (Romans 9:21) In objectifying people, such theology leaves us with a Father as likely to maim and kill his children as save them.

Jesus encountered this misunderstanding. One day, he and his disciples encountered a man blind since birth. The disciples asked, "Rabbi, who sinned, this man or his parents?" They were convinced his affliction was a curse from God. Jesus replied, "Neither this man nor his parents sinned, but this happened so that the work of God might be displayed in his life" (John 9:1–2). The disciples wanted to interpret the man's blindness as a sign of God's wrath. Jesus saw God's presence not in the blindness but in the healing.

Making God both the cause of blindness and the source of healing is dangerous theology. Munchausen-by-proxy is a condition in which a parent secretly harms his or her child in order to garner the attention and praise for the child's care and healing. When humans do this, we call it a mental illness. Yet, like the disciples, we often attribute this very behavior to God. God becomes the source of evil and pain but cleverly redeems himself by healing the very ones he has stricken.

Human brokenness is not the result of God's wrath, but the reason for God's grace. His will is not to break some pots into shards or cast some children into hell. God heals, he doesn't destroy. He welcomes, he doesn't reject. He delivers, he doesn't damn. The potter does more than redeem us from the rubbish pile. With a deft touch, he shapes all his children into something useful and beautiful.

Paul wrote, "For those God foreknew he also predestined to be conformed to the likeness of his Son, that he might be the firstborn among many brothers. And those he predestined, he also called; those he called, he also justified; those he justified, he also glorified" (Romans 8:29–30). I ignored this verse when I thought it a defense of God's favor for a select few. Then I realized, regardless of what Paul intended, it proclaims God's desire to glorify all his children. Our Father, who formed us in the womb, foreknew every one of us and predestined us for glory. I discovered Paul, Augustine, Calvin, and John MacArthur were right about predestination.

God has chosen whom he will save. Their error was in vastly underestimating the number.

This is a common mistake. It plagued the early church and was the cause of Peter's vision. The first Christians didn't understand God's desire to reach the world. They easily adopted Israel's claim of being uniquely favored and chosen. Secure in their own status as children of God, they were willing to allow others to live outside of God's concern. Rather than reaching out to the world, they huddled in Jerusalem.

Both Hebrew and Christian Scripture oppose this arrogance and apathy. Jews were told, "It is too small a thing for you to be my servant to restore the tribes of Jacob and bring back those of Israel I have kept. I will also make you a light for the Gentiles, that you may bring my salvation to the ends of the earth" (Isaiah 49:6). Christians were told, "This is a trustworthy saying that deserves full acceptance, that we have put our hope in the living God, who is the Savior of all men, and especially of those who believe" (1 Timothy 4:9–10).

It is too small a thing to redeem only a few. God wants us all. This good news deserves our full acceptance. Thomas Merton wrote, "A happiness that is sought for ourselves alone can never be found: for a happiness that is diminished by being shared is not big enough to make us happy."[3] A heaven reserved for a chosen few is a heaven too small to bring us happiness. All God's children must be accounted for, every seat at the table taken. Empty seats would be cause for sorrow, a sad reminder of evil's triumph. Only when the table is full can the celebration begin. Only then will God's joy be full.

Those who believe this first are especially responsible to proclaim it to everyone else. Our experience of God's love should be so overwhelming we can't help but share it. When we reserve God's grace or resent God's benevolence, we reveal our desire for favor rather than responsibility, for status instead of service, and for a position at the head of the table. We are like those who sat outside the banquet and complained that Jesus was eating with sinners. Our hope is not in the living God but in our self-righteousness.

I confess my initial rejection of predestination wasn't because it diminished the love of God. I was offended by how such theology undermined my pride. If my salvation were predetermined, how could I boast? I liked thinking I'd "worked out my salvation with fear and trembling." I had chosen God, accepted Christ, and become a member of the Church. I'd picked the right horse. Everyone had the same choice, and if they chose poorly, they deserved damnation.

I ridiculed those who suggested God didn't want to save every person, but I never recognized that my pride in choosing God was equally ridiculous. I suggested God wanted to save every person but couldn't. God wasn't hostile or apathetic toward the lost. God was simply powerless. I raised the banners of divine holiness and justice to excuse God's failure, but my true passion was for human freedom. I insisted we were free to reject God's grace. It never occurred to me that God might be free to reject our rejection.

The Freedom of God

I once considered human freedom the most persuasive argument against the salvation of every person. My friend asked, "How can you believe God would send his children to hell?"

I replied, "God doesn't send anyone to hell. They send themselves. God simply respects their freedom."

Human freedom was the linchpin of my theology. We were saved not by grace, but by our decision to accept God's grace. I argued that though grace is a gift, it must be unwrapped. Though God's grace was for all people, only those who accepted the gift could enjoy its benefits. I thought God's mercy and compassion were reserved for those who, like me, responded quickly and correctly. Grace, when rejected, was withdrawn.

I suppose this conviction grew out of the many times the Church suggested my salvation hinged on my immediate decision. I was reminded in sermons that "today is the day of salvation" and that I must "choose this day whom you shall serve." My life teetered between heaven and hell. God had graciously thrown me a rope, but my failure to grab that rope would spell my doom.

God's grace was usually limited and qualified.

God would be gracious, if I accepted Jesus as my Savior.

God would be gracious, if I was baptized the right way.

God would be gracious, if I attended the right church.

God would be gracious, if I prayed the right prayer.

God would be gracious, if I obeyed the right set of rules.

God would be gracious, if I got it right.

I paid homage to God's grace while championing human freedom. Salvation was not dependent on God's decision to save me, but on my decision to accept him. My righteousness determined my status and destiny. I controlled my destiny. I chose whether I was loved and accepted or hated and rejected. God's love was dependent upon my behavior. Grace was not a gift but a trophy.

I had easily rejected predestination's claim that the

trophy was randomly awarded. What good was a trophy if you hadn't earned it? Though I was uncomfortable when the power to save or damn lay solely in God's hands, I had no qualms with suggesting the power lay completely in mine. In retrospect, my defense of human freedom was simply plain, old human pride. I wanted to take credit for my choice to respond to God's grace. I wanted to believe I chose God.

I remember years ago when a church in our town began an evangelism campaign with billboards, bumper stickers, and buttons emblazoned with the words *I Found It*. The hope was that people would ask what you'd found and you could reply with "Jesus Christ."

At the time, I thought it a clever ploy. Now I realize the bumper stickers misrepresented the human condition. The problem isn't that God is lost and we have to find him. It's just the opposite. We are lost and God has sought us. Jesus said, "The Son of Man came to seek and save what was lost" (Luke 19:10).

When I upheld human freedom, I implied my acceptance of God determined my destiny. Now I believe God's love for me assures my future. I once gloried in the statement "I accepted Christ." Now I celebrate the even better news, "God accepted us." Jesus made it clear to the disciples who did the choosing: "You did not choose me, but I chose you" (John 15:16).

Jesus was equally skeptical of our efforts to save ourselves. He didn't come to disclose a secret formula whereby some might be saved. He came to proclaim the Lord's favor, the good news that all are loved and accepted by God. He made this clear when he took a scroll in the Nazareth synagogue and read, "The Spirit of the Lord is on me, because he has anointed me to preach good news to the poor. He has sent me to proclaim freedom for the prisoners and the recovery of sight to the blind, to release the oppressed, to proclaim the year of the Lord's favor" (Luke 4:18–19).

Jesus didn't believe we were free. He described us as prisoners, oppressed and blind. He didn't suggest our salvation depended on our own ingenuity. He saw us as in need of redemption. Jesus said elsewhere, "I tell you the truth, everyone who sins is a slave to sin" (John 8:34). Jesus saw us as slaves in need of rescue.

We too easily mistake our limited choices for authentic freedom. We are like jail inmates glorying in their freedom to choose their dinner vegetable, oblivious to the guard in the corner and the bars on the window. We exult in our supposed freedom, when in truth we are shackled by selfishness and entangled in evil.

Every decision we make is influenced by our hopes and impaired by our fears. Would I have made the decision to accept Christ if I had been free of my parents' encouragement, the Church's subtle threats, and my over-riding desire to belong? Is any decision, for good or ill, completely free? No one can deny that decisions have consequences, but how much credit can I take for my good choices, and how much blame is due for my failures?

I once thought Tony and I had been presented with the same gift—one I accepted and he rejected. Now I know none of us are as free as we believe and that some are more bound than others. God's grace came to me wrapped in shiny paper, tied in a bow, with a tag bearing my name. My decision to unwrap God's gift came easily. When grace was offered to Tony, his life experiences led him to fear even touching the box. His fears were legitimate. As a young child, he'd watched his father pour hot grease on his mother's arm when breakfast wasn't ready. After all the times Tony had yearned for love, only to be disappointed when it exploded in his face, how could he easily embrace it?

The day will come when Tony will unwrap the gift and know what it means to love and be loved. His fear and resistance are not the final word. Once he truly experiences God's grace, his resistance will end. I hope he will cease resisting on this side of the Jordan, but I am confident he will one day respond. No one who truly understands God's grace will reject it. To do so would be a sign not of freedom but of insanity.

Unfortunately, we live in an insane world. People continually reject God's grace. One reason is that it is so often presented in ugly packages. Too often the Church, which was called to proclaim and extend God's grace, has perverted the message. We've made grace a reward for good behavior, a gift with strings attached. Our attempts to manipulate, control, and limit grace have diminished its appeal. Fear and anger cause the rejection of grace far more than apathy and disdain.

Liberating people to hear the good news is the ministry of the Church. In so doing, we imitate Jesus, whose sermons, parables, healings, exorcisms, and miracles were intended to soften our resistance to God's grace. Jesus said, "You will know the truth and the truth will set you free" (John 8:32). Here is truth: God loves us and is committed to our redemption. To know this is to be released from guilt, fear, anger, bitterness, immaturity, and sin. Thus freed, we are able to receive God's grace and be transformed.

In my obsession with defending human freedom, I forgot a far more important truth: God is free. Though I'd long been persuaded of God's desire to save every person, I continued to think God incapable of such mercy. I argued vehemently for the power of God. I defended God's power to act supernaturally, to split seas and move mountains. I shared Job's conviction that God "can do all

In word and deed, my mother demonstrated her freedom to respond to my hatred with love. Her persistence was evidence of her love. Years later, I would hear myself repeat her words to my children: "Your hate can't change my love." My commitment to love my children prevented me from rejecting them. It was a commitment rooted in my confidence in love's power to overcome hate.

Hate is impotent in the face of such love. When slapped on one check, it offers the other. When forced to walk one mile, it gladly walks another. It may be nailed to a cross, but it cannot be destroyed. It can be attacked, but it cannot be ignored. Love bears all things. This unconditional love will not let us go, even though we would wrench ourselves from its grasp.

Jesus thought conditional love neither impressive nor divine. He said,

> If you love those who love you, what credit is that to you? Even sinners love those who love them. And if you do good to those who do good to you, what credit is that to you? Even sinners do that. And if you lend to those from whom you expect repayment, what credit is that to you? Even sinners lend to sinners expecting to be repaid in full. But love your enemies, do good to them, and lend to them without expecting to get

anything back. Then your reward will be great, and you will be sons of the Most High, because he is kind to the ungrateful and wicked. Be merciful, just as your Father in heaven is merciful. (Luke 6:32–36)

God's love is without condition. He does not accept us because we are good. God is good, loving, and merciful and therefore accepts us. We are free to resist the grace of God, but we are not free to separate ourselves from God's love.

I know this to be true of my relationship with God because I know it to be true of my relationship with my son. Were my son to run away from home, he would separate himself from my blessing. I couldn't feed him. I couldn't clothe him. I couldn't protect him. I couldn't hold him, comfort him, or tell him I loved him. My ability to bless him would be limited, at least until his return. But while my son is free to separate himself from my blessing, he isn't free to separate himself from my love. I have chosen to love him no matter what. His freedom to separate himself from my blessing doesn't diminish my freedom to love him. His freedom to disregard my love doesn't require me to disown or destroy him.

In Jesus' story of the prodigal son, the son was free to leave. He turned his back on his father and his brother.

His departure separated him from the father's blessing. He ended up eating and sleeping with the pigs. Yet neither his departure nor the resulting condition altered his father's love. The son returned, not to a bolted door, but to a welcoming father. His choices and behavior were irrelevant to his father. Before he could make his carefully prepared repentance speech, his father was dressing him in his finest robe. God glories in such homecomings.

This doesn't mean the prodigal's repentance speech was insignificant. Only when he "came to his senses" did he realize his misery and recall his father's love. Only then did he turn toward home. Repentance will always remain a necessary human response to grace. We can be embraced only when we turn into God's arms. God will be satisfied only when we begin to love as we are loved.

Thomas Merton wrote, "Unselfish love that is poured out upon a selfish object does not bring perfect happiness: not because love requires a return or reward for loving, but because it rests in the happiness of the beloved."[4] God gloried not simply in the return of the prodigal, but in his transformation.

Heaven won't be populated by the unrepentant, but neither will hell be anyone's final destination. Like the prodigal, we may wander afar, but we'll ultimately return to the Father. We will freely repent and turn toward home. This turning will signal the end of our resistance.

God's love will be the reason, not the reward, for our repentance.

Augustine said, "You have made us for yourself, and our hearts are restless until they find their rest in thee."[5] This shouldn't surprise us. We were created as children of God. Intimacy with God is the fulfillment of all we seek. God knows we will return home because God knows how we're made. We are free to resist, but our resistance will only remind us of our need. Respecting and expecting our freedom to explore many foreign lands before we turn toward home, God waits patiently. The more we resist, the more miserable we'll become. The more miserable our existence, the more open we finally become to grace. Our freedom, which for so long only brought us pain and misery, will finally bring us joy.

Until that day no choices we make and nothing we do can alter God's attitude. Philip Yancey, a popular Christian evangelical writer, wrote, "There is nothing we can do that will make God love us more. There is nothing we can do that will make God love us less."[6] Poor choices and behavior can destroy our lives, but they cannot force God to destroy us.

Paul wrote, "I am convinced that neither death nor life, neither angels nor demons, neither the present nor the future, nor any powers, neither height nor depth, nor anything else in all of creation, will be able to separate us from the love of God that is in Jesus Christ our Lord" (Romans 8:38–39). Nothing in all of creation can separate us from the love of God. Not even us.

Resisting Grace

God has chosen to save us. Unfortunately, many of us continue to resist and reject God's grace. Some of us are victims of such evil we doubt God's existence or love. Others make such bad choices we believe ourselves beyond God's reach. Some of us think we can save ourselves. Others think salvation unnecessary. Though I believe resistance is ultimately futile, it is hardly irrelevant. Our resistance to the grace of God is the cause of both the evil we experience and cause.

I often wonder why God couldn't have created a world in which resistance was impossible. Thomas Talbott suggests that if we believe God is good, we must assume God created the best of all possible worlds.[7] The best possible world is therefore one in which rebellion and resistance are human options. Of course, if we believe God is good, the best possible world would also have to be a world in which God was capable of overcoming this rebellion and resistance. Creating a world in which evil would ultimately triumph would be an evil act. We are left with this conclusion: rebellion and resistance are real obstacles to God, but they are not invincible.

Our resistance, though powerless to diminish God's affection or ultimately thwart God's will, saddens God deeply. Jesus shared this sorrow while looking upon Jerusalem. Deeply grieved by Israel's resistance to grace, he lamented, "O Jerusalem, Jerusalem, you who kill the prophets and stone those sent to you, how often I have longed to . . ." What did Jesus long for? Did he long for the punishment and damnation of the wicked? No, he longed to gather them together, as a hen gathers her chicks under her wings, but they were unwilling (Matthew 23:37).

I understand that desire to gather someone under your wing. Julie was six years old when she first marched into worship, took a seat in the front pew, and made her presence known. She lived next door to our church with her parents and three brothers. Her family was loud, obnoxious, foul mouthed, and violent. Their fights often burst out of the house and into the street.

I didn't invite Julie to church. She came on her own. Honestly, I didn't want her there. I was certain she'd disrupt our service. I was right. On that first Sunday, Julie got bored during the sermon and crawled underneath the pews from the front to the back. No one remembers my sermon, but everyone remembers our first Sunday with Julie.

Julie came Sunday after Sunday. Several women in the church took it upon themselves to sit with Julie and to keep her off the floor. They encouraged her to listen and to participate. So Julie looked for every opportunity to speak. She always had some joy to share and some concern for prayer. I learned not to pose rhetorical questions in my sermons. On the Sunday I asked, "Have you ever felt unloved?" Julie stood and said, "I have."

Fortunately, she didn't feel that way at our church. We learned to love Julie. One couple bought her dresses for church. Another couple took her shopping for school clothes. At Christmas Julie received more cards than anyone in church. She was still loud, but she was less and less obnoxious.

I suspect Julie came to our church so faithfully to escape her abusive home. Often you could hear one of her parents screaming at her as you walked by the front of the house. Many of us suspected the abuse didn't stop with horrible words. When Julie was fifteen, her parents abandoned her and a younger brother. Her mother went to Florida. Her father took off to North Carolina.

Julie came to live with us.

It seemed the obvious thing to do. We loved Julie. We took her into our home and tried to give her all she had lacked. We gave Julie her own room. We fed her nourishing meals and filled her dresser with clothes. We took her to the dentist. We went to meet all her teachers at school. The only thing we didn't give her was the complete freedom to which she'd grown accustomed.

For three months we focused all our time and energy on Julie. She spent those months rejecting our love, breaking our rules, and looking for somewhere else to live. Near the end, she spread the rumor my wife had hit her. We had to ask her to leave.

Julie was unable to receive our love and resisted our grace.

Whenever I talk about the ultimate triumph of grace, I remember my experience with Julie. While I am convinced of God's eternal love, infinite patience, and gracious persistence, I am equally aware of the reality of human resistance. Indeed, our resistance is what makes God's grace so necessary. "Where sin increased, grace abounded all the more" (Romans 5:20). Grace is God's tool in the continuing creation of the best possible world.

My experience with Julie also reminded me of the difficulty of persevering in grace. I wish my grace had lasted more than three months. While some of our friends said we were saints to have persisted that long, I couldn't help but feel our love had failed Julie. Of course, what will ultimately save Julie is not my patience but God's patience, which never ends. It is God, and not I, who will ultimately save Julie.

My experience with Julie makes me sympathetic to doubts about the power of grace. Why did Julie resist the grace she so desperately needed? Why didn't grace overwhelm her resistance and transform her? Why does that happen to some and not to others? Is the flaw in them or in God's grace? Some believe if we can resist God's grace now, why not for all eternity? They insist grace can ultimately be rejected, that many have done it and are consequently doomed to hell.

I believe our resistance to grace is not proof of God's inadequacy but evidence of the very real obstacles within us to experiencing his grace. Salvation is not the rescue of those who are most responsive. God does not call off the search after finding those in a yellow lifeboat shooting off flares. God seeks those tossed by the sea and clinging desperately to debris. God continues the search long after others have given us up for dead.

Harry is one of the most conservative and compassionate Christians I know. We have had lengthy conversations about my "liberal" theology, and Harry fears for my soul. I do not fear for his. Harry is far more gracious than his theology.

Harry has a wide witness in the lives of many people. He takes every opportunity to tell of God's goodness and love. He creates these opportunities by caring for people in whatever ways he can. While I don't share his conservative theology, I treasure his compassionate heart. We talked recently after he attended the funeral of a man who had died of cancer. Harry had befriended the man and done work around his house when the man was no longer able. He had witnessed to the man up until his death with no apparent success. At the funeral, the grieving widow pulled Harry aside and asked, "Harry, do you think my husband is in heaven?"

I asked Harry what he answered.

He said, "I told her the truth. I told her that when her husband was lying in that hospital bed unconscious and hooked up to all those machines, I prayed for him. The doctors are always saying people can hear more than we think, so I took his hand and asked him to repent of his sins and accept Jesus as his personal Lord and Savior. I told his wife that I believe Jesus was with her husband in those final moments before he died, and I have every reason to hope that he accepted the Lord."

Harry gave the widow the most gracious reply his theology allowed. He portrayed God as graciously persistent. Harry's God was willing to redeem a person even if that redemption came with the very last breath. But, sadly, Harry's God is powerless in the face of death. Those who resist until their dying breath are forever doomed. Death always has the final word.

I believe God has the final word.

Sadly, this has not been the witness of the Church. Though we argue for immortality and celebrate the resurrection, our confidence in the gracious power of God has ended at the grave. When I officiated at funerals for the "unsaved," I once thought their death a great tragedy. God was grieving another child lost for eternity. Death, rather than God, seemed victorious in countless lives.

I can remember many altar calls where the preacher reminded us that "man is destined to die once and after that to face judgment" (Hebrews 9:27). I still agree with that order—death, then judgment. Yet even this sequence makes it clear that death doesn't have the final word. The judge does.

I once thought judgment a frightening prospect. I imagined myself standing before a stern-faced magistrate intent on my punishment. The good news is that we don't face a hanging judge. The judge is our father. In earthly courts, a father would excuse himself from judging his child as a conflict of interest. He'd recognize that his love was bound to influence his judgment.

In the heavenly court, there will be no conflict of interest. God's love will influence his judgment. He will not don his black robes and forget who we are. He may chastise. He may express his disappointment. He may even punish. But his final word will be a redeeming word of grace.

To sentence his children to eternal torment would make a mockery of God's love and power. Theologian John A. T. Robinson said, "Judgment can never be God's last word, because if it were, it would be the word that would speak his failure."[8]

The Southern Baptist preacher Clarence Jordan wrote,

> I just cannot stick my God into a little time-space relationship here, hindered and always working against the impending physical death. . . . Maybe God is in hot pursuit of us; we've been thinking of giving our heart to Christ. We're thinking so hard on it we're driving along and we don't hear the whistle of a freight train. And bam . . . it just smashes us to pieces. And God said, "You know, I almost had him. That freight train beat me to him." What kind of a God is that? A God whose purposes can be voided by a freight train? I can't fit that in.[9]

Neither can I.

I believe God wants to, can, and will save every person. Human resistance is real and persistent, but God's grace will ultimately wear down every obstacle. God is patient because even death cannot thwart God's desire.

This good news is what Christians celebrate every Easter. It's why I find the story of Jesus so compelling. In Jesus, grace is lived, tested, and triumphant. He proclaimed the persistence of God's love. Those who opposed his message challenged, persecuted, and ultimately killed him. Convinced death was the final word, they thought he and his message silenced. Yet the death of Jesus was not the final word. An empty tomb, and not the cross, is the heart of the gospel.

1. John MacArthur, *The God Who Loves: He Will Do Whatever It Takes to Draw Us to Him* (Dallas: Word, 1996), 127. When I read this title, I had such hopes. What I find perplexing is that MacArthur argues God will not do whatever it takes.

2. MacArthur, *The God Who Loves,* 130.

3. Thomas Merton, *No Man Is an Island* (New York: Harcourt Brace Jovanovich, 1955), 3. This quote is from an essay titled "Love Can Be Kept Only by Being Given Away." I consider it one of the finest essays on love ever written.

4. Merton, *No Man Is an Island,* 3.

5. Augustine, *Confessions.* Unfortunately, Augustine thought some hearers would remain forever restless.

6. Philip Yancey, *What's So Amazing About Grace?* (Grand Rapids: Zondervan, 1997), 70. One of the best books ever written on grace. He simply failed to write the final chapter.

7. Thomas Talbott, *The Inescapable Love of God* (Parkland, FL: Universal Publishers, 1999), 174–80. Talbott argues a world where some are damned cannot be the best possible world.

8. John A. T. Robinson, *In the End God* (London: James Clark, 1950), 106.

9. Clarence Jordan, *The Substance of Faith* (New York: Association Press, 1972), 150. This quote is from his wonderful sermon titled "God's Destination for Man."

Five

The Salvation of God

I believe God will *save* every person.

I was recently interviewed by a newspaper journalist. I spent two hours sharing my experiences with the grace of God, extolling the loving character of God, and explaining how this love motivates God's desire to save every person. I told the stories and made the arguments you've been reading.

A week later the newspaper article ran with this opening sentence: "Local writer and pastor no longer believes Jesus is the only way of salvation."

Though I don't recall using those exact words, I can't fault the reporter for coming to that conclusion. If you believe God loves and will save every person, you can't claim redemption as an exclusively Christian experience.

Salvation is no longer the sole possession of a specific culture, religion, denomination, or person. Salvation belongs to God. It is what God does in the lives of all his children.

The response to the newspaper article was quick and angry. The editor of the paper was inundated with negative letters. Many wrote me directly. I was attacked and scolded. Some damned me to hell while others sought my repentance. I tried to be gracious in all my replies. I understand their reaction. The reason I didn't come right out and say, "Jesus isn't the only way," is because those words are still difficult for me to say or hear. They seem blasphemous. People always assume I'm demeaning Jesus.

That's not my intention. I still claim Jesus as Lord and Savior, though I understand discipleship and salvation differently. I believe Jesus had a special relationship with God and an important role in human history, though I'm no longer persuaded this required his divinity. I'm committed to living the way of Jesus, though I no longer insist "there is no other name under heaven given to men by which we must be saved" (Acts 4:12). I value the cross and the resurrection, though they have new meaning. My understanding of Jesus has changed.

I resisted this. When I became convinced God would save every person, I tried to hold on to traditional Christian formulas—the trinity, the incarnation, and atonement theology. I wanted to pour this new wine into old wineskins. I quickly learned why Jesus recommended against this: the old wineskins always burst. Just as fermenting wine causes old leather to rend and tear, my expanding view of God strained the credibility of my childhood theology. As Oliver Wendell Holmes Jr. once said, "The mind, once expanded to the dimensions of larger ideas, never returns to its original size."

My mind enlarged, I had to abandon formulas I'd been taught, had preached, and had defended. I'd insisted only those washed in the blood of Jesus would be saved. Salvation was a cosmic negotiation between Jesus and God. I'd been convinced only those who practiced my faith pleased God. Salvation meant belonging to the Church. I'd been certain only Christians would enter heaven. Salvation was reserved for those who claimed Jesus as the way, the truth, and the life.

It wasn't easy leaving those old wineskins behind. Ironically, the most critical letters helped the most. They allowed me to hear the ideas and language that were becoming offensive to me. Warnings that I'd "burn in hell" and demands that I "return to the narrow way" exposed the inadequacy of fear and conformity as religious motives. Being on the receiving end of Christian "evangelism" for the first time, I discovered why it often fails. It lacks grace. It demands others adopt its formula or else!

One letter was especially enlightening. The writer expressed her deep disappointment in me, quoted a few Bible verses, and ended by asking, "Without Jesus, who will pay for your sins?" Her question provoked another question, one I'd never heard or asked: Why must sins be paid for? If God is forgiving, why is any payment necessary? I was forced to examine deeply ingrained ideas and unquestioned assumptions.

Atonement, or payment for injury, is one such age-old idea. It is a theme in many religions and philosophies and is embedded in Jewish and Christian theology. It's easy to defend in Christian tradition and Scripture. It resonates with our human obsession with justice. We may doubt the grace of God, but we're convinced that sins—especially those of our enemies—must be atoned.

There is one major problem with atonement theology. It contradicts the ethic of Jesus. Jesus rejected the demand for "an eye for an eye, a tooth for a tooth." Rather than demanding payment for injury, he commanded us to turn the other cheek. Jesus championed grace and ridiculed the meticulous justice keeping of his religious peers. He offered forgiveness so freely that, when he forgave the sins of a paralytic, his opponents complained, "This fellow is blaspheming!" (Matthew 9:3) In any culture obsessed with balanced scales, grace will seem blasphemous.

As I've said, I once found the salvation of all scandalous. It offended my sense of justice. It didn't bother me that God only forgave after the debt had been paid. I never questioned why a God who demanded his pound of flesh on a blood-drenched cross should be considered gracious. Only when I began to take grace seriously did such ideas make me uncomfortable. I found it more and more difficult to sing, "What can wash away our sins? Nothing but the blood of Jesus." Eventually, those words no longer made sense to me. The forgiveness of sin didn't require the death of Jesus. It only required God's resolve to forgive. Grace isn't about Jesus' paying for our debts. It's about God's removing our transgressions, as far as the east is from the west.

The Problem with Atonement

When I was young I accepted Jesus as my Savior. I don't regret that decision. In following Jesus, I was saved from self-absorption. I learned the joy of being loved and loving others. I was freed from the obsessions that so easily entangle and ruin our lives. What I regret was being taught that Jesus died in order to save me from the hands of a wrathful God.

This was unfortunate and untrue. Long before Jesus, God said, "I, even I, am the Lord, and apart from me there is no savior. I have revealed and saved and proclaimed" (Isaiah 43:11–12). From the beginning, God chose to save his children.

The first story in the Bible tells of the creation of the world. God creates earth and moon, land and sea, plant and animal, fish and fowl, and finally human beings. "God saw all that he had made, and it was very good" (Genesis 1:31). It's a wonderful story with one major flaw. The world we know doesn't fit this description.

The second story in the Bible tries to explain the discrepancy. It tells of human rebellion. It exposes the human desire to be God rather than be in relationship with God. It acknowledges the consequences of human sin. Finally, it reveals God's response to our rebellion and sin: God doesn't destroy us.

The story of Adam and Eve is a story of grace. God had warned, "You may freely eat of every tree of the garden; but of the tree of the knowledge of good and evil you shall not eat, for in the day that you eat of it you shall die" (Genesis 2:17, RSV). But when they disobeyed and ate, they didn't die. They were forced to leave the Garden, but God was gracious. "The Lord God made garments of skin for Adam and his wife and clothed them" (Genesis 3:21). God continued to care for them.

The third story of Genesis is even more surprising than the second. Cain murders his brother Abel. Surely murder is the ultimate test of grace. How does God respond to such evil? Again, the reality of evil isn't denied. Cain is forced to face the consequences of his sin and is banished from his family. Yet God doesn't destroy Cain. In fact, God places his mark of protection on him and leads him to a new land. God doesn't destroy his children even when we are rebellious and wicked.

Unfortunately, this grace hasn't been the foundation of most Christian theology. The theology of my childhood argued just the opposite. God was angry. My sin offended him. He demanded justice. My debt had to be paid. God sat in heaven, scales in hand, scowling as my sins tipped the balance closer and closer to wrath. God was bent on my destruction.

Such thinking reflects another story in Genesis. In the story of Noah and the flood, God looks down on earth and says, "I will wipe mankind from the face of the earth for I am grieved that I have made him" (Genesis 6:7). This was not the God who made clothes for Adam and Eve and promised Cain his protection. This God had murder in his eyes. I've come to believe the first stories of Genesis reflect one of the oldest theological debates, one that runs through the rest of the Bible and divides us today: Does God save or destroy?

Unfortunately, for thousands of years, those convinced of God's malevolence have carried the day. In the ancient world, this resulted in the killing of animals to appease a host of angry gods. When the blood of bulls and lambs wouldn't suffice, human slaves and prisoners were slaughtered on altars. In 1486, at the dedication of the Great Temple in Tenochtitlan, the Aztecs killed twenty thousand people in one day to honor their war god. Many cultures eventually sacrificed their own children in order to satisfy a bloodthirsty god. Most ancient peoples believed divine favor could be purchased only in blood.

Both Judaism and Christianity accepted this assumption with little critique. Judaism, though rejecting the sacrifice of humans, still adopted this view of the cosmos and approach to salvation. God kept Abraham from killing Isaac, but a ram still had to die. This God said, "The life of a creature is in the blood, and I have given it to you to make atonement for yourselves on the altar; it is the blood that makes atonement for one's life" (Leviticus 17:11). Only blood could atone for sin and restrain the wrathful hand of God.

Early Christianity, influenced by its Jewish roots, interpreted the death of Jesus through this same lens. Jesus was the sacrificial lamb who atoned for the sins of the world. Rather than emphasizing the love of the Heavenly Father, early Christians portrayed God doing precisely what he forbade Abraham to do: God sacrificed his son. Though rejecting the efficacy of animal blood, Christianity defined salvation as the result of human sacrifice. "Without the shedding of blood there is no forgiveness" (Hebrews 9:22). Only in the death of Jesus was God's wrath satisfied.

This is a stark explanation of a much more complicated theological argument, but the basic premise is clear. Traditional Christian theology has argued God is grieved he made us, seeks our destruction, and forgives only after the debt is paid. Jesus saves us from God. Grace, rather than being an expression of God's love, becomes a grudging willingness to forgive and favor those washed in blood.

Long before I believed in the salvation of every person, I was uncomfortable with blood theology. As a teen, I was appalled by a church with an actual fountain spurting blood-red water. It reminded me of some B horror movie. In seminary, I worked hard to emphasize the symbolic and metaphorical aspects of the atonement. During communion, I tried to extol the life-giving dimensions of blood. In the end, it didn't work. I found a forgiveness that depended on the shedding of blood repellent.

I no longer believe salvation requires blood, a sacrifice, or the payment of a debt. I'm in good company. Neither does God. Hosea proclaimed, "I desire mercy, not sacrifice, and acknowledgment of God rather than burnt offerings" (Hosea 6:6). Isaiah prophesied, "The multitude of your sacrifices—what are they to me? I have more than enough of burnt offerings, of rams and the fat of fattened animals; I have no pleasure in the blood of bulls and lambs and goats" (Isaiah 1:11). David said, "You do not delight in sacrifice, or I would bring it; you do not take pleasure in burnt offerings. The sacrifices of God are a broken spirit; a broken and contrite heart, O God, you will not despise" (Psalm 51:16–17).

Jesus was equally skeptical of blood atonement. "To love God with all your heart, with all your understanding and with all your strength, and to love your neighbor as yourself is more important than all burnt offerings and sacrifices" (Mark 12:33). Love, rather than blood, was the source of forgiveness and relationship.

When salvation requires a sacrifice, forgiveness and grace become commodities to be bought rather than gifts of God. More troublesome, Jesus ends up saving us from God rather than from evil. Jesus shields us from a vengeful God rather than leading us toward abundant life. When I was a teen, a youth leader explained, "Salvation is Jesus picking up the check for the whole room." The problem with such analogies is they portray God as a stingy accountant unsatisfied until every penny is paid. Jesus is glorified at God's expense. Jesus is gracious and God is a coldhearted scrooge.

Suggesting God required Jesus to pay the debt is equally confusing. Is a God who only forgives after an innocent man is tortured and killed a God worthy of praise? Atonement theology, with its insistence on balancing the scales and sustaining the ancient fear of divine malevolence, refuses to allow God the freedom to simply cancel the debt. It ultimately contends that unless blood is shed, God is powerless to forgive.

Fortunately, this isn't the only understanding of salvation. Some biblical accounts never mention blood at all. They suggest Jesus revealed what has always been true: God is our Savior. "When the kindness and love of God our Savior appeared, he saved us, not because of the righteous things we had done, but because of his mercy. He saved us through the washing of rebirth and renewal by the Holy Spirit, whom he poured out generously through Jesus Christ our Savior, so that, having been justified by his grace, we might become heirs having the hope of eternal life" (Titus 3:4–7). *Kindness, love, mercy, rebirth,* and *renewal* are words of grace. *Sacrifice, blood,* and *debt* suggest forgiveness given grudgingly at best.

Forgiveness doesn't rely on sacrifice, blood, or the payment of debt. Forgiveness has always been the choice of God. God was as gracious prior to the cross as God was after the cross. The death of Jesus didn't enable God to forgive, nor did it change God's mind about us. God has never sought our destruction, but our completion. Jesus wasn't born to die. He came to teach us how to live. Jesus didn't die to appease an angry God. He came to proclaim a God of love.

Obviously, rejecting blood atonement creates a new set of questions. Why did Jesus die? What is the meaning of the cross? How do we understand the resurrection? How can we continue to speak of Jesus as Savior? What does it mean to be saved? I continue to believe the events that transpired in Jerusalem nearly two thousand years ago were the acts of a gracious God. I also fear that for the past two thousand years we've missed the point.

The Cross and the Empty Tomb

Rebecca was enthusiastic until I challenged the cross.

When I asked her about her experiences with God, she gushed with story after story of God's goodness. When I suggested everything God does is motivated by love, she quickly agreed. When I shared my conviction that God will save every person, she thought it wonderful news. When I admitted I didn't believe Jesus died for our sins, she was shocked. She asked, "Then why did Jesus have to die?"

The simple answer is, he didn't. His death was not God's will. God didn't send Jesus into the world to atone for sin. He was born to live, learn, and know God. He experienced a profound intimacy with God. Around the age of thirty, Jesus felt led to challenge the inaccurate images of God prevalent in his day, to introduce people to his Father, and to encourage them to live as people of grace. Jesus hoped the people of Israel would respond to his message and become "a light unto the Gentiles." What Jesus sought was not the establishment of a new religion, but the establishment of the kingdom of God—a kingdom of goodness and grace.

Unfortunately, as Jesus discovered, only a few glimpsed this kingdom. Most, rather than sharing his vision, thought him demon possessed. His insistence on the grace of God when many were eagerly awaiting God's wrath only increased their suspicion. Rather than raising an army to challenge Rome, he cleared the temple and claimed its courts as "a house of prayer for all nations" (Isaiah 56:7). Instead of destroying the Gentiles, he invited them into the Holy of Holies. Grace got Jesus killed.

Jesus died because the clash between unwavering love and unyielding pride and intolerance always result in a cross or an assassination or torture or imprisonment or persecution. The cross is simply one more sign of humanity's consistent resistance to grace. We silence any messenger who challenges our quest for a favored position.

Calvary was not the fulfillment of a divine plan. It was not the final installment on a cosmic debt. It was not necessary to satisfy some bloodthirsty deity. The crucifixion was the cost of proclaiming grace. The more insistent Jesus was on God's grace, the more likely was his eventual death on the cross. His death was a human act rather than a divine sign. People, not God, demanded his crucifixion.

We don't like to admit that. There was a hymn we sang when I was a child called "Who Killed Jesus?" Each verse named a different suspect. The first blamed the Roman soldiers, the second accused Pilate, and the third charged the Jewish people. The final verse concluded that we killed Jesus. Jesus opened his arms to embrace the world, and we nailed his outstretched hands to a cross.

Of course, we all want to believe we'd have acted differently. We wouldn't have followed orders or washed our hands of guilt or cried for his blood. We read the Gospel accounts of political and religious leaders plotting and killing Jesus but fail to recognize that their actions represent humanity's typical response to grace.

When I was growing up, I remember how scornful preachers and teachers were of the Pharisees. Only after I had studied Judaism and spent years in the pastorate did it occur to me that the Pharisees sounded remarkably like the most rigorously religious people of our day. They were sanctified, law abiding, Bible believing, and ritual keeping. When I was most honest about who best represented my attitudes and opinions in the Gospels, I had to identify with the Pharisees. They sounded like me. People like me, resistant to the blind generosity of grace, killed Jesus.

This doesn't make the cross meaningless, but it alters its significance. The cross, no longer understood as a payment for human sin, illustrates human resistance to grace. But more than that, it reminds us of the cost of being gracious in an ungracious world. Jesus said, "If anyone would come after me, he must deny himself, take up his cross, and follow me" (Luke 9:23). When we suffer for insisting on God's love for all, the crucifixion reminds us we are in good company, and our ability to experience suffering with hope and joy is increased.

Of course, this is small consolation if the crucifixion is the end of the story. A dead Jesus, falsely accused and unjustly killed, would be as much a reason to despair as to hope. In focusing on the cross, Christianity has missed the point. We've been so morbidly fascinated by the crucifixion we've failed to appreciate the true symbol of our hope—the resurrection. The death of Jesus is not the final word. The final word is undying love.

Without the resurrection, Christianity is an empty husk. It is merely another sad story of a good man defeated by evil and humiliated in death. Paul wrote, "If there is no resurrection of the dead, then not even Christ is raised. And if Christ has not been raised, our preaching is useless and so is your faith" (I Corinthians 15:13–14). My faith is in a risen Christ.

This may surprise you. I'm often asked how I can continue to believe in the resurrection of Jesus after questioning so many other stories in the Bible. The resurrection of Jesus is one of the more incredible claims of Scripture. Any fair reading of the Gospel accounts must admit to uncertainty about the nature of Jesus' resurrection. In some accounts, he seems a ghost. In others, he can be touched and he eats fish. In a few, he isn't initially recognized. The specifics of the resurrection are fuzzy at best.

On the other hand, the Gospels are also brutally honest about the attitude of Jesus' disciples immediately following his death. They weren't eagerly anticipating his return. They were in hiding, depressed and discouraged. They were as skeptical of the women's reports of an empty tomb as anyone. Yet something transformed this band of peasants and fishermen. Something inspired their message of resurrection. Many of them died with that testimony on their lips and that hope in their hearts. They believed Jesus lived.

So do I. I can't claim a visitation like the early disciples or a vision like Paul. Even Jesus suggested such appearances were uncommon. He said, "Because you have seen me, you have believed; blessed are those who have not seen and yet have believed" (John 20:29). I am one of those who hasn't seen and yet believes. My belief in the resurrection doesn't depend on the authenticity of the Shroud of Turin. It doesn't rely on the inerrancy of the Bible. For me, and for millions, it is a matter of faith. I believe in the resurrection because it is consistent with what I've experienced of God. Life, not death, is God's design for his children.

God did something glorious in Jesus. His resurrection settled once and for all the question of God's attitude toward his children. God has determined to love and redeem. In the crucifixion we said no to God, but in the resurrection God rejected our rejection. This is the triumph of grace.

God has never been undecided about our destiny. He has not been waiting for an appropriate sacrifice or for our acts of contrition or for our cries for mercy. God does not need to be appeased, and he does not require a scapegoat. Jesus did not have to die on a cross in order for us to be forgiven. He did not do what God was unwilling or unable to accomplish. He did not convince a reluctant

God to be merciful or ransom sinful people from the wrath of God or die to satisfy the requirements of justice.

Jesus revealed what has always been true—God is our Savior. He is the one who created us. He is the one who sustains us. He is the one who redeems us from death and claims us as his own. Paul wrote, "This grace was given to us in Christ Jesus before the beginning of time, but it has now been revealed through the appearing of our Savior, Christ Jesus, who has destroyed death and has brought life and immortality to light through the gospel" (2 Timothy 1:9b–10).

The Revelation of Jesus

For many years, I've considered Jesus my Savior. When I first became convinced of the salvation of every person, I argued that every person would eventually accept Jesus as Savior. My formula for salvation remained unchanged. I simply believed every person, either before or after death, would ultimately bow to Jesus.

I wasn't able to maintain that position very long. Paul wrote, "Love never insists on its own way" (1 Corinthians 13:5, RSV). I realized insisting that every person must eventually come to know God in precisely the way

I had wasn't gracious. It was the same arrogance that branded Galileo a heretic.

In 1632 Galileo published a book challenging the time-honored way people perceived the world. Within months he was summoned to Rome and put on trial. He was found guilty of heresy and was forced to kneel in front of the Inquisition and recant. To refuse would have meant his death. Even after he recanted, he was condemned to life imprisonment without contact with the outside world. The Church feared he might infect others with his heresy. He died, blind and alone, in 1642. His heresy? He believed the earth was not the center of the universe with the sun, moon, stars, and other planets rotating around it. In 1992, over twenty years after men walked on the moon, the Church finally admitted to having erred in dealing with Galileo.

I understand why Galileo's thoughts were so threatening. We want to believe we sit at the center of God's universe. I was reluctant to surrender Jesus as the only means of salvation. I wanted to believe the Christian story was the center of the religious universe. Every religion had some of the truth, but Christianity was the total package. I had to accept that many spiritual expressions rotate around what is truly central: the grace of God.

The grace of God was the message of Jesus. Unfortunately, I had become so enthralled with the messenger that I neglected the message. It's an easy mistake to make. I heard of a woman who was so excited on receiving a long-awaited letter that she kissed the mailman. She wanted to express her joy in a tangible way to a flesh-and-blood person. I can sympathize with her desire. I can also understand that mailman's surprise and discomfort.

My friend Tracy is in prison. He committed a crime, admitted his guilt, and was sentenced to thirty years. When he was first arrested, he called from jail and asked me to visit him. He was depressed and suicidal. I began to visit with him weekly and tell him of God's love and forgiveness. One day I had the honor of praying with him as he finally believed in this love. He's been a changed man ever since.

Tracy often says, "Thank you so much. You saved my life."

That always makes me uncomfortable. I always reply, "No, Tracy, God saved you."

He always answers, "I know that, but you were the one who showed me God's love."

My experience with Tracy gave me new insight into the role of Jesus. It is God who saves us, but for many it was Jesus who visited us in our captivity, when we were discouraged and without hope, and showed us God's love. This is why the early church claimed Jesus as Savior. It wasn't that Jesus died for our sins and saved us from the hands of an angry God. Jesus revealed the saving grace of God.

In this sense, Jesus saved me from my misconceptions about God. He saved me from my fear of being rejected. He saved me from my needless and fruitless efforts to earn God's favor. He saved me from any anxiety over God's ultimate intention for my life. Once I understood his message of grace, I was freed from the power of evil and sin. I began to love as I had been loved.

Jesus said, "When a man believes in me, he does not believe in me only, but in the one who sent me. When he looks at me, he sees the one who sent me" (John 12:44). In Jesus, I saw God. He was tangible, flesh and blood, the incarnation of grace.

I use the term *incarnation* carefully. I don't use it to describe a quality unique to Jesus. I simply affirm what I and many others have experienced—the word became flesh. The scholar Huston Smith wrote,

> Jesus went about doing good. He did so with
> such single-mindedness and effectiveness that
> those who were with him constantly found their
> estimate of him modulating to a new key. They
> found themselves thinking that if divine good-
> ness were to manifest itself in human form, this
> is how it would behave.[1]

I am reminded of the story of a little boy who was afraid of the dark. He was afraid of the monsters he thought lived under his bed and in his closet. His parents would pray with him every evening and ask God to protect him, but he would always end up in their bed.

One night his father said, "You don't have to be afraid. God will be here in your room with you."

The little boy answered, "I was hoping for someone with skin."

My friend Tracy began praying the first night he was thrown in jail. I believe God was with him every moment and comforted him in ways he was unaware of. I also believe God sent me to be "someone with skin." What I accomplished on a small scale, Jesus did for many. He was an incarnation of God. He was one who revealed God's salvation.

His goal was not to draw attention to himself, but to point to the source of all love—his Father in heaven. Many experienced the presence of God in him. Yet he didn't claim this quality of relationship for himself alone. He prayed, "I have given them the glory that you gave me, that they may be one as we are one" (John 17:22).

This is why I use the term *incarnation* carefully. I'm not suggesting Jesus was 100 percent man and 100 percent God. Even when I believed that, I couldn't explain or understand it. Neither am I arguing Jesus was biologically human and spiritually divine—God wearing a human costume. I now believe in something far more wonderful. God was present in Jesus in the same way God wishes to be present in all of us. He wants to fill us with his spirit— to make us into people of grace.

Was God uniquely present in the life of Jesus? I don't think so. Even Jesus was uncomfortable with people's attempts to make him unique. In the Gospels, Jesus often discouraged those who called him the Son of God or the Messiah. This is usually interpreted as a sign of humility or of pragmatic necessity. I've begun to suspect Jesus was wary of such attention. Once, a man addressed Jesus as "Good Teacher." Jesus replied, "Why do you call me good? No one is good but God alone" (Luke 18:19). Jesus went out of his way to discourage adulation.

On another occasion, while Jesus was traveling, a woman in the crowd called out, "Blessed is the mother who gave you birth and nursed you." He responded, "Blessed rather are those who hear the word of God and obey it" (Luke 11:27–28). Jesus was far more concerned with people's understanding the grace of God than with their adoring him.

This is not to diminish the significance of Jesus. In Jesus, God was present in a powerful way in a particular time for a specific purpose. Jesus revealed the grace of God. His attitude toward the world was God's attitude. His desire to seek and save the lost reflected God's desire. His willingness to heal and forgive was God's will. His life demonstrated the way God intends to redeem the world. His death demonstrated the strength of his conviction. His resurrection confirmed his message of grace.

I still consider Jesus my Savior, but not for the same reasons I once did. Neither do I assume everyone comes to a knowledge of God's grace through Jesus. I am discovering God has used men and women who didn't even know the name of Jesus to communicate the same message as Jesus. Jesus said it this way: "Whoever is not against you is for you" (Luke 9:50). Those who live gracious lives follow the way of Jesus and please God.

I've become far less obsessed with celebrating Jesus' death and far more interested in living his life. I once claimed him as Savior; now I seek to make him Lord. I share Paul's desire. "I want to know Christ and the power of his resurrection and the fellowship of sharing in his sufferings, becoming like him in his death, and so, somehow, to attain the resurrection from the dead" (Philippians 3:10–11). I want to walk the way of salvation.

The Way of Salvation

One day, Jesus met a man named Matthew. He was a tax collector. He wasn't an IRS auditor, as much as we may dislike them. The tax collectors of that day were more like the Mafia. They were allowed by the Romans to collect as much as they could as long as Rome got its cut. The Jews hated them. Matthew had daily contact with Gentiles, which made him religiously unclean, and he worked for the Romans, which made him a traitor.

Jesus, disregarding Matthew's pariah status, befriended him, invited him into his inner circle, and ate dinner with him and his friends. This violated religious and social boundaries, drawing the ire of religious folk of Jesus' day. They asked his disciples, "Why does your teacher eat with tax collectors and 'sinners'?"

On hearing this, Jesus responded, "It is not the healthy who need a doctor, but the sick. Go and learn what this means, 'I desire mercy, not sacrifice.' For I have not come to call the righteous, but the sinner" (Matthew 9:11–13).

In these three sentences, Jesus defined his ministry and his vision of salvation. He divided humanity into two groups: those who have been rejected and those who believed themselves righteous. He offered mercy to the rejected and challenged the righteous to be merciful. He implied both groups needed salvation.

Ironically, both the rejected and the righteous have misunderstood the grace of God. The rejected assume their "sinful" behavior has removed them from God's affection and desire. The righteous conclude their "goodness" has assured them God's love and favor. Both groups have defined their relationship with God by their behavior rather than by God's character and will. In that sense, both groups are self-absorbed.

It's a common mistake. I met my friend Steve when he was in prison. When he came to our Bible study, his first words were, "Don't tell me God loves me because I don't believe in God." Hostile and confrontational, he tested my patience week after week. I made certain each week to seek him out before I left and tell him I loved him.

Eventually, Steve told me his story. His was a childhood designed to produce a serial killer—neglect, abuse, abandonment, and hate. This treatment had produced his rage and self-destructive behavior. It also explained why he doubted God's love. Where was God in the midst of his misery? Hearing his story also changed how I perceived him. I began to see what Jesus saw in Matthew the tax collector. He and I saw men who had confused human rejection for the attitude of God.

The only cure for this sickness is love and acceptance. Jesus told Matthew, "Follow me." I told Steve I loved him. Matthew responded immediately. Steve took more time, but eventually his hostility abated and he reconsidered both his disbelief in God and in God's love. One day Steve sidled up to me and said, "Don't take this wrong. I don't want to have sex with you or anything, but I love you too." I consider this the day of Steve's salvation.

No longer was his relationship with God defined by the evil done to him or the sins he'd committed. He found mercy instead of judgment. Steve had assumed his crimes assured God's rejection. When he discovered his behavior couldn't alter God's attitude toward him, he was saved.

Steve was one of those who thought themselves rejected. I was one who considered myself righteous. Steve thought his actions had made God love him less. I was convinced my behavior had made God love me more. We both needed salvation.

I remember the first time Ronnie, a former prisoner, invited me to attend a worship service at the jail. I made some poor excuse. When Ronnie persisted, I began to avoid him. I had no desire to enter a prison. Eventually Ronnie asked me, "Haven't you read in the Bible where Jesus says, 'I was in prison and you visited me'?" He challenged my behavior, and since my salvation depended on my behavior, I went with him to the jail one Sunday night. Obligation rather than love motivated me.

Attending that jail service transformed me. I went in as a righteous one fulfilling his obligation to minister to the rejected ones. I left that evening more fully aware of God's love for me. My transformation came as I stood before those men and said, "God loves you. He loves you regardless of what you've done. Indeed, the more terrible your actions, the more persistent his love." Those words became real in my life even as I spoke them.

I discovered the meaning of salvation. Salvation comes with believing God loves you unconditionally. It is abandoning the misconception that you are rejected because of your bad behavior or accepted because of your goodness. Only when we repent of this self-absorption and focus on God's love can this love alter us. Then and only then can God transform hearts darkened by sin and soften hearts hardened by self-righteousness.

It is from this self-absorption that we must be saved. Often, when I speak of my belief in the salvation of every person, someone will object that without the threat of hell, people would sin wantonly. They consider the possibility of eternal punishment as the only deterrent to human selfishness. Unfortunately, if this is true, even serving God and loving our neighbor become acts of selfishness. Self-absorbed choices, by their very nature, separate us from God and from others.

I learned this from Jesus.

One day, Jesus was teaching when an expert on the law stood up to test him. The expert asked, "What must I do to be saved?"

Jesus didn't hold an altar call. He didn't lead him through the four spiritual laws. He didn't baptize him. He didn't ask him to subscribe to a specific creed. He didn't even suggest the man believe in him. He asked, "What is written in the law?"

The man answered, "Love the Lord your God with all your heart and with all your soul and with all your strength and with all your mind and love your neighbor as yourself." In other words, don't be self-absorbed.

"You have answered correctly," Jesus replied. "Do this and you shall live" (Luke 10:25–28).

This was not the only time Jesus suggested that salvation is a result of abandoning our obsession with self and living in love. He gave a similar reply to the rich young ruler when he asked what he must do to be saved. Jesus suggested that if he wanted to be perfect, he must sell everything and give the money to the poor. Even Jesus' disciples were scandalized by this response. Salvation was no longer a matter of belonging to the right group or keeping the right rules, but of denying the self and practicing mercy.

On another occasion, Jesus was dining with a Pharisee named Simon when a woman of ill repute came to him. She wet his feet with her tears, wiped them with her hair, kissed them, and poured perfume on them.

Simon was appalled by this woman's presence and actions. He was even more shocked by Jesus' willingness to allow such a woman to kiss him.

Jesus said to Simon, "Do you see this woman? I came into your house. You did not give me water for my feet, but she wet my feet with her tears. You did not give me a kiss, but this woman, from the time I entered, has not stopped kissing my feet. You did not put oil on my head, but she has poured perfume on my feet. Therefore, I tell you her many sins are forgiven—for she loved much."

Then Jesus looked at the woman and said, "Your faith has saved you; go in peace" (Luke 7:44–50).

What did the woman have faith in? I believe she had faith in Jesus' willingness to love and accept her. She no longer feared rejection or condemnation. She had caught a glimpse of the grace he preached and lived. She responded and experienced salvation.

Oddly, the way Jesus spoke of salvation differs from the salvation language eventually adopted by the Church. Salvation became a matter of believing in Jesus rather than understanding what he taught. Salvation was in Jesus' name rather than through his way. Those initially called the followers of the Way became known as Christians.

The Jesus portrayed in John's Gospel parrots the exclusive thinking that developed quickly in the early church. Jesus says, "I am the way, the truth, and the life. No one comes to the Father except through me" (John 14:6). No longer was the emphasis on following his way, a way of grace, forgiveness and love, or accepting his truth, the truth that we are all loved by God, or living his life, a life dedicated to reaching out to even the most unlovable. My friend Ray says, "The problem with Christianity is we made it into a religion about Jesus rather than a commitment to be like him." We lost our way.

The message of Jesus—that salvation is a matter of abandoning self-absorption and being transformed by the love of God—became obscured. Within two hundred years, salvation would mean believing "Jesus was the only begotten son of God, begotten of the Father before all worlds, God of God, Light of Light, begotten not made, being of one substance with the Father, by whom all things were made" (Nicene Creed). We were no longer saved from our self-absorption. We were saved from the sin of not believing certain things about Jesus. Those who believed these things were saved, and those who didn't were damned. Whether people lived the way of Jesus became irrelevant to some and secondary to many. Salvation became a status, easy to achieve and verify. This misunderstanding persists.

Occasionally people knock on my door or hand me a tract on a street corner or strike up a conversation with the aim of asking, "Are you saved?" Even before I believed in the salvation of every person, I always answered with an enthusiastic yes.

Often, rather than sharing my elation, my inquisitors would look me up and down with a dubious eye and ask another question. The second question varied depending on the person. Many asked, "Have you repented of your sins and accepted Jesus as Lord and Savior?" Some asked, "Do you belong to a Bible-believing church?" Others asked if I'd been fully immersed or baptized in the name of Jesus or filled with the Holy Spirit and spoken in tongues. My salvation hinged on how I answered their second query.

Those most aggressive about determining my salvation were also most certain what it meant to be saved. They knew the sole formula. Claiming to be a Christian was never enough. I had to subscribe to their specific explanation for the human condition, the activity of God, the means and purpose of salvation. If not, I faced damnation.

I could mock the exclusive claims of such people, but for years I shared their arrogance. I didn't knock on doors, hand out tracts, or ask people if they were saved, but I too thought myself a gatekeeper in the house of

God. When others believed and acted as I did, I threw open the gates and celebrated their salvation. When they didn't, I barred the door. I was annoyed when someone questioned my spiritual condition but blind to how their attitude mirrored my own. My formula, although more tolerant and inclusive than some, did not include all.

Only after I abandoned my post as a gatekeeper did I begin to understand salvation differently. No longer was salvation about finding the key or learning the magical password to the locked gates of heaven. Salvation became a process rather than an event and a means rather than an end. It was a journey toward gates that will never be closed.

Salvation is turning away from self-absorbed lives. It is trusting in our acceptance by God. It is allowing the knowledge of God's love to transform our opinion of ourselves and others. It is beginning the journey home. It is accepting that we are saved by grace

Though there have been significant milestones in my spiritual journey, my salvation has been a process. God has been removing my obstacles to intimacy through the power of his grace. This grace is transforming me from what I was into what I shall be. Salvation is my journey from estrangement from God and others toward divine and human communion.

This process continues in my life. In the beginning I doubted my salvation. Slowly I become convinced of God's love. I came to believe in God's love for those like me. Yet there remained millions to whom I denied any common experience or any relationship with God. Fortunately, the God who has been saving me from self-absorption continued to allow his grace to work on me. He brought people into my life who challenged my narrow understanding of salvation. He helped me face the last great sin.

The Last Great Sin

One day when Jesus was traveling through Samaria on his way to Jerusalem, he sought refreshment in a village. They refused to welcome him. "When the disciples James and John saw this, they asked, 'Lord, do you want us to call fire down from heaven to destroy them, even as Elijah did?' But Jesus turned and rebuked them. He said, 'You do not know what kind of spirit you are of, for the Son of Man did not come to destroy men's lives, but to save them'" (Luke 9:54–55).

Since the very beginning, the disciples of Jesus have tried to destroy the opposition. Instead of patiently awaiting the transformation of others, we've quickly divided the world into "us" and "them." We haven't even re-served this distinction for those of other religions. We're intolerant of any deviation from the party line. Catholics thought Protestants apostate and damned. Protestants re-turned the favor, then splintered into a variety of denom-inations. Many of those knocking on doors and sending missionaries overseas remain convinced their version of the Church is the only true Church.

This exclusive understanding of salvation has its comforts. It allows us to feel special, righteous, and part of the "in" crowd. However, in an increasingly pluralistic world, remaining comfortable with theological exclusiv-ity is more and more difficult. A Christian zealot is no less aggressive than a Muslim, Hindu, or Jewish zealot. Meet-ing people as arrogant as we are—convinced they're spe-cial, righteous, and saved while we're not—is threatening enough. More disturbing are encounters with gentle, humble, compassionate people who understand salvation differently. What if they're right and we're wrong?

Most of us ignore that question. Limiting our inter-actions to those like us is one cure for discomfort. An-other is to redouble our efforts to recruit more disciples to our group. There is strength in numbers. When de-nominations announce their membership or religions count their adherents, they imply numbers are an assur-ance of salvation. We're hoping a billion Christians or

Muslims or Buddhists can't be wrong. We grow nervous when we hear of another denomination or religion growing faster than ours. In the past this anxiety became violent as religions resolved to convert the competition at any cost, even genocide.

Unfortunately, salvation as recruitment continues to drive most religion. The crusades of this age have been in large stadiums rather than battlefields, but the motive remains the same. We remain confident of our salvation and the damnation of others. This sin is characteristic of nearly every religious group. It motivates Mormons to knock on the doors of church parsonages, inspires Christians to send missionaries to Israel, and even justifies Muslims flying airplanes into skyscrapers. Instead of asking ourselves why there are gentle, humble, gracious people in every religious tradition, we seek to recruit or destroy them.

We are uncomfortable with the thought that God might be at work in all the world, in all people, and even in all religious systems. Sadly, I've discovered that traditional Christianity, Islam, and Judaism share one common belief—they are certain God won't save everyone. Those who knocked on my door or handed me a tract on the street suspected I wasn't saved. In recent years, when I've confessed that I believe everyone will be saved, I've confirmed their suspicions. They thought my belief in the salvation of everyone a sure sign of damnation.

My unwillingness to believe in the salvation of all of God's children was my last great sin. It allowed me to think myself self-righteous and others damned. It excused my apathy toward many and my hatred of some. It kept me from completely believing in the salvation of God. As long as some of my brothers and sisters were doomed, how could I be secure in God's love?

When I repented of my insistence that God save some and damn others, I was freed to live my life graciously. No longer was my life obsessed with comparing myself with others or with striving to earn God's favor. I began to experience the incredible joy of knowing someday every person will know the love I know.

Salvation is not the hope of a few; it is the destiny of all.

1. Huston Smith, *The World's Religions* (San Francisco: HarperSanFrancisco, 1991), 324. This is one of the finest books on comparative religions ever written.

S i x

The Persistence of God

I believe God will save *every person.*

Whenever I share my belief in the ultimate salvation of every person, I am invariably asked, "You mean every person? You mean Christians and non-Christians? You mean people who don't even believe in God? You mean people who've done horrible and evil things? You mean Hitler is going to be in heaven?"

The answer is yes. I mean the whole world, every person who has been, is, and shall be. I mean Muslims, Hindus, Buddhists, Jews, New Agers, pagans, and Christians. I mean atheists, agnostics, the apathetic, and the hostile. I mean the rapists, child molesters, and terrorists. I mean the person you or I think the most evil, most despicable human on earth. I believe God will save us all. We will all repent and be transformed.

Heaven will be populated by people of every nation, race, and creed. God's children, in all of their diversity, will be seated around his table. They will have two things in common. They will have the same Father, and they will have been redeemed and transformed by the same grace. This grace will humble the exalted and exalt the humble. We will call every man our brother and every woman our sister. Those damaged and hardened by evil will be healed and renewed. Hell will be empty.

It's taken me many years to empty hell. As a child, I was taught only Christians would be saved. Billions of non-Christians would crowd hell. The thought of non-Christians in eternal torment didn't disturb me because I'd been told Christians were good people and non-Christians were bad people. Since I grew up in a Midwestern American town where nearly everyone belonged to a Christian church, I had little opportunity to test this assumption. Non-Christians lived in the big city or in foreign countries—the places where we sent missionaries.

I remember the first time I seriously questioned this worldview. I was in college when I saw the movie *Gandhi*. I walked out of that theater forever changed. In Gandhi, I encountered a good man who was also a non-

Christian. In fact, his commitment to love and mercy far exceeded that of many Christians. While he never acknowledged Jesus as Savior, he lived the way Jesus commanded us to live.

Suspicious that Hollywood had glamorized Gandhi, I read many of his writings and what others wrote about him. The more I read, the more I admired him. His words and actions reminded me of Jesus again and again. Gandhi said, "I believe in God, not as a theory, but as a fact more real than that of life itself."

One day I shared my admiration for Gandhi with a friend.

He responded, "Isn't it sad that he's burning in hell?"

His statement shocked me. Yet I quickly recognized how traditional Christian formulas assign Gandhi to eternal torment. Since he never accepted Christ, he must burn in hell. When I would protest the injustice of a good man being eternally punished, I was reminded that we don't get to heaven because we are good but because we've accepted Christ. Gandhi, having rejected Christ, was damned for all eternity.

Even before I believed in the salvation of every person, I struggled with this injustice. I found it impossible to accept that those living the way of Jesus were damned for not taking the name of Jesus. Assigning Hitler to hell was easy. Unfortunately, most Christian formulas suggested Hitler shared the same hell as the Jews he murdered. They too hadn't accepted Jesus as Lord and Savior.

Ironically, Hitler's desire to purge humanity of those he thought impure and deficient is the extreme manifestation of what many religions affirm—that some people ultimately deserve annihilation. He damned millions to concentration camps and furnaces, convinced he was purifying the world. He did on earth what many expect God to do in the afterlife.

Later, I would discover something even more disturbing than the damnation of Gandhi and other good non-Christians. I realized many Christians destined for heaven weren't good people at all. They were hateful, vindictive, greedy, dishonest, and immoral. Many in the Gestapo attended church regularly. Some who claimed the name of Jesus were wicked.

I remember hearing John Calvin's idea of the invisible Church. He argued that we can never judge who is or isn't part of the Church. Only God knows those who have sincerely repented and followed Christ. I found this a wonderful solution to my quandary. I decided Gandhi and many others were members of this invisible Church and many within the visible Church weren't members at all. This allowed me to reserve hell for the truly wicked.

Fortunately, I eventually moved to the big city. I became a pastor among the "wicked" and found my judgment of people as either good or bad less and less defensible. I remember sitting in my office one day when Betty came to see me. She told me that she'd decided she was ready to join the church. I cringed.

Betty was a worn woman who lived in a broken-down house with five large dogs, several cats, her homosexual son with AIDS, and a man to whom she wasn't married. She was a mess. What would people think if we allowed her to join our church? Instead of welcoming her, I told her she needed to get her life together. She needed to become a good person.

Betty went away sad. She never again asked to join us. Over the next few years, I ran into Betty time and again. She was always gracious to me. She was often carrying some animal she'd found abandoned, which she'd care for until she could find it a home. Other times she was returning from helping some neighbor. When the woman down the street came down with cancer, Betty spent hours caring for her. I learned one day that one of her children was severely handicapped and that she drove a hundred miles to visit him nearly every week.

She, like many others I've described in this book, challenged my easy judgments about who is good and who is bad. I discovered fewer and fewer people were truly wicked. My reservation list for hell continued to shrink. Hell became the destiny of those who'd committed themselves completely and totally to evil—Adolph Hitler and the like.

Then I became involved in prison ministry. I remember the day I was preaching at the jail and realized one of the faces was familiar. It was a man who I'd read about in the newspaper. He'd sexually abused his child and then killed him. When it came time for prayer requests, he rose and tearfully asked us to pray for God to work in his life. I was shocked that God was still at work in this wicked man. Didn't some deeds require God to turn away?

Did I really want someone like him to repent, find forgiveness, and be transformed? Didn't Hitler deserve to be thrown into the fire? I once would have happily allowed them to burn. That no longer brings me joy. The only fire I desire for the wicked is the purifying fire of God's love. Thomas Talbott writes, "Once the consuming fire of God's love has destroyed, whether in this life or in hell itself, everything that is false within us, once nothing of the false self remains for us to cling to, then nothing of our opposition to God will remain either."[1] The only fire Hitler requires is the fire of divine love, which will consume the dross of his hatred and evil, leaving him humbled, repentant, and seeking his proper place in the divine order.

I don't know how long this purifying will require for

Hitler and for me, but I am confident in God's patience. Peter said, "The Lord is not slow in keeping his promise, as some understand slowness. He is patient with you, not wanting anyone to perish, but everyone to come to repentance" (2 Peter 3:9).

The more patient I've become, the less easily I've assigned people to hell, the less I've wanted some to perish, and the more I've desired the repentance of everyone. Much of my impatience was a result of underestimating God's persistence. I thought the catch, the small print on the contract, was that God's promises applied only until death. Those resistant or unrepentant or ignorant until death were damned. Grace was temporary.

Recently, I was flipping through the radio and heard an urgent appeal: "Today could be your last day. Don't miss out on what could be your final opportunity! No one knows when the doors will be shut and locked forever. This offer could end tomorrow."

Those words reminded me of sermons I once preached, but it turned out to be a furniture store's annual going-out-of-business sale. Unfortunately, for too long I believed grace was also a limited-time offer, that one day God would be out of the grace business. With death God ceased to be our loving father and donned the robes of an impartial judge. Those cast into hell were forever lost.

I don't believe that any longer. The psalmist wrote, "Whither shall I go from your spirit? Whither shall I flee from your presence? If I ascend up into heaven, thou art there: if I make my bed in hell, behold, thou art there" (Psalm 139:7–8, KJV). God seeks us even though we would make our bed in hell.

God's love is eternal. It does not end at our death. God's patience is infinite. It is not merely for this life. God's grace is persistent. It endures beyond the grave. I believe God is, has always been, and will always be gracious.

Grace Beyond the Grave

The idea that grace endures beyond the grave is what troubles people. When I speak of God's love, everyone is pleased. When I argue for God's patience, most are comforted. When I tell of God's persistence, some are moved to tears. When I suggest that God's love, patience, and persistence never end, many become angry.

One woman said, "I've worked hard to live a good life, and now you tell me everyone is going to get in."

I don't have much sympathy for such a response. Such self-righteousness offended Jesus, who spoke tenderly to sinners but reserved his harshest words for those who gloried in their own goodness.

Her response may have been the kind that generated one of Jesus' most scandalous stories.

Jesus compared God to "a landowner who went out early in the morning to hire men to work in his vineyard" (Matthew 20:1). The landowner hired men at dawn, then at the third hour, the sixth hour, the ninth hour, and the eleventh hour. When the day ended the landowner paid each of the workers the same wage. Those who signed on at dawn were indignant at the landowner's unfairness.

The landowner replied, "Friend, I am not being unfair with you. Didn't you agree to work for a denarius? Take your pay and go. I want to give the man who was hired last the same as I gave you. Don't I have the right to do what I want with my money? Or are you envious because I am generous?"

Then Jesus said, "So the last will be first, and the first will be last" (Matthew 20:13–16).

Why are we so bothered by extravagant grace?

If God should choose to bless all the "workers," shouldn't that be a cause for celebration, not for anger? His grace is so wonderful we should covet it for all. Why do we resent those who've discovered the blessing long after we have? We shouldn't resent them. We should grieve that some are the last to discover his grace. We should rejoice that we who were first can join God in welcoming the last.

Who are the last?

The last are those people who still have not understood God's love for them. They are the last to respond, the last to repent, the last to turn toward home, the last to take their seat at God's banquet table. When the last take their place, we should welcome them gladly.

When will the last come home?

Obviously, it will not be in this life. There is no evidence Adolph Hitler repented of his evil prior to killing himself. There are too many instances in which people we know and love seem to resist God's grace to the bitter end. There are far too many stories of young, rebellious people cut down in the prime of their life.

When will God finally redeem the last person? I don't know. I'd like to believe that once a person is freed of this life and fully aware of God's love, all will be transformed. But perhaps not. C. S. Lewis, in his book *The Great Divorce,* suggests some will continue to resist even after death. He describes hell as a city populated with people convinced of their own righteousness and sufficiency. He imagines a bus traveling from hell to heaven each day. Those in hell are always welcome to visit heaven. They are met by saints who try to encourage them to stay. Most quickly board the bus for the return trip to hell.

The first to return to the bus is a man convinced

there must have been a mistake. He's met in heaven by one of his former employees who was convicted of murder. Terribly offended, he says, "What I'd like to understand is what you're here for, as pleased as Punch, you, a bloody murderer, while I've been walking the streets down there and living in a place like a pigstye all these years."[2]

The saint who was once a murderer freely admits his sin and tries to explain God's grace, but the man from hell will have nothing of it. He is convinced a great injustice has been done. He complains, "I'd rather be damned than go along with you. I came to get my rights, see? Not to go sniveling along on charity tied to your apron strings. If they're too fine to have me without you, I'll go home."[3] He gets back on the bus.

I share Lewis's hunch that the most resistant may be the self-righteous. Those who've sinned terribly are often the most receptive to grace. My fear is that if hell exists it will be populated with people like the man C. S. Lewis described—Christians offended by grace. The last may be those who complain of God's extravagance.

Whatever the case, I'm convinced God's eternal love will overcome even the hardest heart. God's infinite patience will exhaust every remnant of rebellion. God's persistent grace will allow God to outlast the resistance of even his most rebellious child. God's grace will never end.

An Eternal Love

I know a man who hates change. He has attended the same church for sixty years. He has sat in the same pew all those years, except for the Sunday I preached a sermon titled "Getting a Fresh View." I began the sermon by asking everyone to move to a different pew.

He hated that sermon.

He fights change tooth and nail. When the music committee bought new hymnals, he refused to sing. When the worship hour was changed, he showed up at the same old time. When the church began a new prayer chain, he insisted on calling the old list.

Needless to say, he hated my sermons on ultimate redemption. I tried several times to visit him and discuss our disagreement. He, though retired, always had other, more pressing, engagements. He finally told me on the phone, "What's the point of talking when you'll never change my mind?"

One of his favorite Scriptures is "Jesus is the same yesterday and today and forever" (Hebrews 13:8).

He told me, "You can change the hymnal. You can change the worship hour. You can change the prayer chain. But you can never change Jesus."

We disagreed about the hymnals, the worship hour, and the prayer chain. We agree about Jesus. I believe

Jesus fully revealed God's gracious nature. I believe this grace is the same yesterday and today and forever.

God's grace is eternal.

The psalmist writes, "I will declare that your love stands firm forever, that you established your faithfulness in heaven itself" (Psalm 89:2). In the second letter to Timothy, we read, "If we are faithless, he will remain faithful, for he cannot disown himself" (2 Timothy 2:13). God could no more disown his children than he could himself.

I remember when I first loved my children. It was not on the day when they climbed into my lap, hugged me, and said, "I love you, Daddy." It was not on the day when they took their first step or babbled "Dadda." It was not on the day they quit crying when I held them. It was not on the day they were born. The first day I loved them was when my wife announced, "We're going to have a baby."

Such is the love of God. God has loved us from the very beginning, while we were yet in the womb. He did not wait to see if we were lovable. He did not require us to earn his love. He did not reserve his love for some and deny it to others. God has loved all of us from the very beginning.

God will love us to the end.

The Hebrew word for God's love, *hesed,* means "steadfast, unfailing love." The psalms declare repeatedly that "his love endures forever." It is this steadfast, unfailing love that is our salvation. "Through unfailing love and faithfulness sin is atoned for" (Proverbs 16:6). Let me be clear: it is not our love and faithfulness that save us, it is God's.

An entirely different word, *'ahab,* is used to describe human love. Human love is not steadfast. It often fails. "Many a man claims to have unfailing love, but a faithful man who can find?" (Proverbs 20:6) This is why God's love requires a different word. To speak of God's love is to speak of an unfailing love.

The New Testament continues the distinction between divine and human love. The Greek word for God's love is *agape.* Paul describes agape in the thirteenth chapter of 1 Corinthians. He ends his description with these words: "Love always protects, always trusts, always hopes, always perseveres. Love never fails" (1 Corinthians 13:7–8). If God's love is not eternal, then we indeed have reason to fear. If God's love can fail, we have no reason for hope.

Thankfully, God has loved us "with an everlasting love" (Jeremiah 31:3). It is this unfailing love that makes it possible for God to be patient. God knows his love will outlast every evil and overcome all resistance. God is patient because God is confident.

Unfortunately, many are not confident of God's patience. They insist there must be a moment when God's patience ends. Indeed, they seem to crave such a day. The Bible is not immune from such talk. A passage in Revelation concerning the end of the world has long troubled me. It reads, "I [John] saw under the altar the souls of those who had been slain because of the word of God and the testimony they had maintained. They called out in a loud voice, 'How long, Sovereign Lord, holy and true, until you judge the inhabitants of the earth and avenge our blood?'" (Revelation 6:9–10)

This passage distresses me because it portrays the saints waiting impatiently for vengeance. I have known people like this in my life, but I never considered them saints. When I think about saints, I think of my friend Johan.

Johan is an active opponent of the death penalty. He testified to the Indiana Senate on behalf of a bill to end capital punishment. His testimony is especially powerful because he holds this conviction despite the brutal murder of his younger sister.

"My sister was only fourteen when she was killed. Tyrone King killed her with a sawed-off shotgun. We know that she did not die right away; she must have been in extreme agony for some time, with part of her abdomen blown away. I hope that King feels remorse— I hope he has twisted in agony himself, thinking of the harm he caused. But even if he feels no agony at all, and is spiritually dead to reality, I know that God is a God of justice and can be trusted to deal with him. I would rather have him alive and laughing about what he did than shortcut God's grace, from which I also have benefited."

I believe the saints are those men and women who love with God's steadfast, unfailing love. They do not eagerly await God's wrath. They anticipate God's grace not only for themselves, but also for those who've wronged them. They await the triumph of grace with great patience.

An Infinite Patience

Impatience is epidemic in our culture. We seethe after thirty seconds of being put on hold. We grumble when our fast food isn't fast enough. We honk when the person in front of us doesn't accelerate immediately at the green light.

While these are minor matters, our impatience is not limited to the trivial. I have seen couples divorce after one session of marriage counseling failed to restore the romance. I have seen children abused by short-fused parents insistent on immediate obedience. I have seen new Christians rejected by a church the first time they backslide.

Impatience is the absence of grace.

When Paul listed the attributes of divine love in the thirteenth chapter of 1 Corinthians, he began with "Love is patient." It is no accident that Paul mentioned patience first. Without patience, love is impossible.

As we become more gracious, we become more patient. We don't seethe so quickly, grumble so audibly, or honk so instantly. We realize that good marriages are years in the making. We see good parents balance tolerance with obedience. We learn good Christians patiently lift up fallen brothers and sisters and dust them off. The practice of patience makes us aware of God's patience and how it far exceeds our own.

How patient is God?

Paul writes, "Christ Jesus came into the world to save sinners—of whom I am the worst. But for that very reason I was shown mercy so that in me, the worst of sinners, Christ Jesus might display his unlimited patience" (1 Timothy 1:15–16).

The unlimited patience of God is the hope of the world.

I can't pretend the Bible is consistent in its portrayal of God. Some stories suggest God is quickly angered, easily frustrated, and terribly impatient. One such story has Moses, after the Israelites have built a golden calf to worship, convincing God not to destroy his stiff-necked people and start from scratch. Moses appears more patient and gracious than God. I am skeptical of that story. I don't believe any human can be more patient or gracious than God.

Infinite patience is beyond our understanding.

I know a woman whose husband had an affair. She forgave him, and over time they restored their marriage. Her friends marveled at her grace and patience.

I asked her, "If your husband had another affair, could you forgive him again?"

She thought for a minute.

She answered, "I don't think so. I don't think I could bear that much pain and offer that much forgiveness again."

Human patience, forgiveness, and grace are limited.

One day Peter came to Jesus and asked, "Lord, how many times shall I forgive my brother when he sins against me? Up to seven times?" (Matthew 18:21)

Peter was trying to impress the Lord. Seven times seemed extravagant to him. In fact, the Jewish rabbinical tradition suggested three times was adequate. In *The Gospel of Matthew,* William Barclay wrote,

In the opening chapters of Amos there is a series of condemnations on the various nations for three transgressions and for four. From this it was deduced that God's forgiveness extends to three offenses and that he visits the sinner with punishment for the fourth. It was not thought that a man could be more gracious than God, so forgiveness was limited to three times.[4]

The rabbis were right in thinking a man couldn't be more gracious than God, but they vastly underestimated God's graciousness. Jesus made that clear when he responded to Peter's attempt at extravagance.

"Jesus answered, 'I tell you, not seven times, but seventy times seven'" (Matthew 18:22). Of course, Jesus was not suggesting that 490 should be the limit of our forgiveness or of God's. Indeed, Jesus went on to tell the story of a man whose debt of millions was forgiven. He was explaining that forgiveness and grace are infinite. They are infinite because God's patience is infinite.

God is patient for a reason. God trusts his patience will finally turn us from our wicked ways and the toll they take. God is patient because he knows his prodigals will one day come home.

In Luke 15 Jesus tells of a father whose youngest son demands his inheritance, runs off to a distant land, and wastes his wealth in wild living. The son ends up sleeping with the pigs, where he comes to his senses and repents. He turns toward home. There is nothing unusual about the son's story. It is the story of millions of sons and daughters.

What made that homecoming exceptional was the heart of the father. Jesus said, "While the son was still a long way off, his father saw him and was filled with compassion for him; he ran to his son, threw his arms around him and kissed him" (Luke 15:20).

The father saw the son coming because the father had been waiting and watching. He expected his son's return.

The purpose of God's patience is our salvation. "Bear in mind that our Lord's patience means salvation" (2 Peter 3:15). To whom does God's patience mean salvation? To everyone.

Some suggest the story of the prodigal son doesn't say the father will wait forever. They're technically right. But I cannot imagine the father Jesus described finally giving up, shutting the door, setting the dead bolt, and turning off the light. A loving father doesn't give up. If he grows impatient, he puts on his coat, leaves a note on the door, and sets out in search for the one he loves.

If God is impatient, he is impatient to redeem.

Perhaps this is why Jesus, in the fifteenth chapter of Luke, explains God's attitude toward sinners with three stories. The story of the prodigal assures us of God's patience. The other two stories proclaim God's persistence.

While God is patient, he is not content to wait. His grace is eternal and his patience is infinite, but he sees and hears the misery of his children. He does not gloat at their suffering or gleefully anticipate the moment he can say, "I told you so." Rather, the cries of his children spur him to seek and save the lost.

A Persistent Grace

Recently, a young girl disappeared. The police initiated a search. The television stations covered the trauma. The newspapers ran daily articles. They found her jacket, but she remained missing. Days turned to weeks and weeks turned to months.

Over time the police spent less and less energy on her case. The television stations moved on to other tragedies. The newspapers found other stories. The hundreds who searched the first weekend gradually returned to their own lives.

Almost everyone stopped looking.

A reporter asked her parents, "When will you stop looking for your daughter?"

They replied, "Never."

Those who love never stop seeking.

I believe God is no less persistent.

The Hebrew Scriptures testify to this persistence. They document thousands of years of God's steadfast relationship with Israel. God's faithfulness was seldom repaid in kind. The story of Israel is one not of a people faithful to God, but of a God faithful to his promise. "He will never leave nor forsake you" (Deuteronomy 31:6). Never.

Jesus recalled that promise when he was preparing to leave his disciples. He told them to "go and make disciples of all nations" and "teach them to obey all that I have commanded." No small commission. Then he added these words of reassurance: "Surely I will be with you always, to the end of the age" (Matthew 28:19–20). Always.

Never and *always* are the words of a persistent God. Some claim these promises were only for Israel or only for the disciples. Some will argue God's persistent grace is only for the chosen—the chosen being a special few of whom the speaker is invariably a member. Fortunately, regardless of what the people of Israel, the disciples, and others may believe, God persists in the lives of all people.

One of the better known verses of the New Testament reminds us, "For God so loved the world that he gave his one and only son, that whomever believes in him should not perish, but have eternal life. For God did not send his son into the world to condemn the world, but to save the world through him" (John 3:16–17). God is not interested in a chosen few. God is devoted to redeeming the whole world, in choosing everyone.

Who can forget the childhood agony of standing in line on a summer's day, waiting to be picked for a game? The captains picked the best athletes first, seeking every advantage, contesting back and forth. Player after player was chosen, while you stood waiting, trying to appear indifferent but wanting the earth to open up and swallow you whole. Finally, only you and another player were left.

"If I take him, you have to take her," one captain said.

Thus, you were chosen. Not with glad shouts and celebrations, nor with pats on the back welcoming you to the team, but with discouraged resignation and grudging acceptance.

Some would have us believe God's acceptance of us is similarly conditional, that he welcomes some with enthusiasm and others with disdain. This misconception is not new. Jesus was often criticized for picking the wrong people, those everyone else would have picked last, if at all. They complained, "This man welcomes sinners and eats with them" (Luke 15:2).

No one would have been critical if Jesus had preached condemnation to these unsavory types. What they objected to was Jesus' eating a meal with them. In Jewish culture, breaking bread together was a sign of full acceptance. Jesus heard them muttering about the company he kept and responded with two pointed questions: "Suppose one of you had a hundred sheep and loses one of them. Does he not leave the ninety-nine in the open country and go after the lost sheep until he finds it?" (Luke 15:4) "Or suppose a woman has ten silver coins and loses one. Does she not light a lamp, sweep the house and search carefully until she finds it?" (Luke 15:8)

The answer to both of these questions is obviously no. None of us would risk the ninety-nine to save the one. None of us would waste money on oil so we would have light to search for one coin. Or, if we did search, it would be for only a short time. None of us would be this persistent.

Jesus believed in a God who seeks the lost until he finds them.

Frederick Craddock notes in his commentary on Luke,

> If the ninety-nine are safe in the fold, then the search for one lost sheep is but an act of frugality,

an exercise in common sense. . . . But how is one to assess the search by a shepherd who leaves ninety-nine in the wilderness? Either the shepherd is foolish or the shepherd loves the lost sheep and will risk anything, including his own life, until he finds it.[5]

Clarence Jordan, in a sermon on the parable of the woman seeking the lost coin, asks,

What does she do? She gets a broom. She sweeps and sweeps and sweeps. She lights a lamp and sweeps until what? Until she wore the broom out? No. Until the lamp went out? No. Until her husband came home and said, "Hey, get my supper, what are you doing with that broom?" No. How long did she sweep? Until she found it. How long was that? As long as necessary.[6]

God will seek, as long as necessary, until he finds us.

This is tremendous news for those who've been taught that death is the final word, that grace is a temporary offer, that eternal punishment awaits those who die without accepting Jesus. God will not be satisfied until every seat at his table is filled.

The Great Banquet

I have often heard heaven described as a grand courtroom. God sits on the throne of judgment. We stand before him with head bowed and knees shaking. The
scenes of our life are replayed before us with every sad
and sorry act revealed for all to see. God prepares to pass
judgment. Those who've repented of their sins and accepted Jesus Christ as personal Lord and Savior will be
pardoned. Everyone else is thrown, begging for mercy,
into the pits of hell. Heaven is a place of judgment rather
than joy, regret rather than repentance, grief rather than
grace.

Fortunately, this is not the only image of heaven in
Scripture. Jesus seemed partial to another description.
He likened the kingdom of heaven to a banquet and told
of a king who said, "'Go to the street corners and invite
to the banquet anyone you find.' So the servants went
out into the streets and gathered all the people they could
find, both good and bad, and the wedding hall was filled
with guests" (Matthew 22:10).

The parable of the prodigal son ends with a similar
celebration. The father, on greeting his lost son, proclaims, "Bring the fattened calf and kill it. Let's have a
feast and celebrate" (Luke 15:23). Jesus seemed convinced heaven would be a party where we will celebrate

not only our redemption, but also the restoration of our lost brothers and sisters.

There was a time when I was more interested in a heavenly courtroom than a divine banquet. I was enthralled by my righteousness. I gloried in God's judgment because I found it so easy to judge those around me. I was an elder son.

The parable of the prodigal son probably should be titled the parable of the prodigal sons. There are two sons in the story. I have already discussed in detail the younger—his descent into sin and his eventual repentance. I have highlighted the gracious response of the father in welcoming home his lost child. I have not said anything about the elder son.

His story is my story. The elder son stayed home. He made no demands, did his chores, and sought to impress his father. He never offered to go look for his younger brother. He was content to bask in his father's good graces. Yet the elder son was far from perfect. When his younger brother returned and his father forgave him without condition, the elder son became enraged. He stomped home to discover a party when he had hoped for a trial. He refused to come in the house, to sit with his brother, to celebrate his redemption. He turned his back on his brother and on his father. In the end, the son with his back to the father resisting grace is the elder son. He becomes the prodigal.

When the father tried to convince the elder son to join the celebration, he responded, "Look! All these years I've been slaving for you and never disobeyed your orders. Yet you never gave me even a young goat so I could celebrate with my friends" (Luke 15:29). His response exposed his heart. His obedience and work were not motivated by love for his father. His hope was that he would be rewarded with a party for himself and a few friends.

I think one of the reasons I resisted the idea of God's saving everyone was that I wanted heaven to be a party for me and a few select friends. I was relying, not on God's grace, but upon my own goodness. I was interested in reward, not repentance. I now realize religion that is primarily motivated by heavenly reward is flawed. It is no more admirable than a man who tells a woman he loves her simply to get her into bed. The elder son's response to grace was my response. Somehow he and I lived in the father's presence without ever appreciating the father's character.

The father responds to this ugly revelation with grace. He says, "My son, you are always with me and everything I have is yours. But we had to celebrate and be glad, because this brother of yours was dead and is alive; he was lost and is found" (Luke 15:32). The father is as gracious to the elder son as he was to the younger. Indeed, he has left the party to seek him. The father cannot celebrate until all his children are around his table.

Jesus doesn't tell us whether the elder son repented and returned to the banquet. There's a reason Jesus doesn't finish the story. He's inviting us to resolve the story. What will we do? Will we turn from God and his grace? Or will we join the party? I have decided to join the party.

Joining the party requires forgiveness. It is that one thing, forgiveness, we elder sons find so hard to accept from God and so difficult to extend to those around us. Yet this is the way of grace. Forgive as you are forgiven. Be merciful as you receive mercy. Love as you have been loved.

We are not to resent the inclusion of all people in God's redemption. Methodist theologian David Lowes Watson writes,

> There are still too many empty places at the banquet table. The appropriate attitude for guests who have already arrived, therefore, is to nibble at the appetizers, and anticipate the feast which is to come. To sit down and begin to eat would be an unpardonable lapse of good manners, especially since the host is out looking for the missing guests and could certainly use some help.[7]

Indeed, the host has asked us to gather all the people, good and bad, into his banquet hall. We are to join God in looking for the missing guests. Paul wrote, "God was reconciling the world to himself in Christ, not counting men's sins against them. And he has committed to us the message of reconciliation. We are therefore Christ's ambassadors, as though God were making his appeal through us" (2 Corinthians 5:19–20).

This work of reconciliation must continue until every last person is redeemed.

I do not know where we will sit at the final banquet, but I suspect who will sit beside us. On our right will sit the person whom we have harmed the most. On our left will sit the person who has done the greatest evil to us. We will be seated between grace received and grace required.

My friend Paul once stood in church and asked the forgiveness of a Japanese woman named Meiko. What made his apology so startling was our knowledge that Paul was a Pearl Harbor survivor. He experienced the Japanese surprise attack that killed over two thousand people. Some of these people were his friends.

Why would Paul ask Meiko for forgiveness?

Paul said, "I've realized in the past months as I sat in the choir and looked out at Meiko every Sunday that I haven't forgiven the Japanese people. All these years I have allowed that bitterness to remain deep in my heart. Today I forgive them and ask Meiko to forgive me."

This is a foretaste of the banquet.

At the great banquet, the only tears will be tears of joy. We will see a fundamentalist Christian embracing Gandhi, a humbled Hitler washing the feet of a Jewish Holocaust victim with his tears, Paul shaking hands with a Japanese pilot, Jesus kissing Judas. The lion lying down with the lamb.

You know who will be seated next to you.

You may complain that I do not understand what they did to you. How cruel and petty and evil they were. How they showed no remorse. You may stomp your foot and refuse to be seated next to them. You may say you can never forgive them.

But then someone will tap you on the shoulder and you'll turn to look into the eyes of someone you hurt. Someone to whom you were cruel, petty, and evil. Someone to whom you never apologized. Someone who has every right to refuse to sit with you. But who will instead say, "I forgive you."

I hope you will find in that grace the power to turn and forgive. I hope you will repent. But even if you do not, I have good news. The party will not start without you. Indeed, you are one the guests of honor. God will wait. The saints and angels will wait. They are in no hurry. Neither am I. We have eternity.

Of course, we'd rather not wait. We'd rather begin the celebration right now. The final challenge is postponing the party until the last guest has arrived. We must find the patience to live in faith, hope, and love. We must be persistent even when evil mocks our confidence.

The Final Challenge

I walked into the emergency room and saw Benny. His face was black and blue, caked in dried blood, his eyes pinched shut, his lips swollen and bleeding. In the middle of the night, two men had broken into Benny's home, beaten him severely, and then robbed him. A terrible thing to happen to anyone, but especially heinous when you know that Benny is a seventy-year-old mildly mentally handicapped man recognized throughout his neighborhood for gentleness and generosity. Even more evil when the detective concluded the thieves knew Benny well enough to know he'd cashed his pension check that day.

In moments such as these, it's hard to believe in the triumph of grace. Evil seems far from defeated. I'm tempted to believe in a salvation that includes everyone but the men who beat Benny. I had to fight my rage as I tried to comfort him. We talked about the attack, his injuries, the good prognosis from the doctor, and then I asked him if I could pray with him.

Benny nodded his head and said, through swollen lips, "Don't forget to pray for those men."

As a pastor, I've been witness to great evil. I've heard it whispered at an altar, confessed in my office, announced in a courtroom, and repented of in a hospital bed. The horrid details of marital infidelity, child abuse and molestation, embezzlement, murder, and rape have all been shared with me. Evil no longer surprises me.

Grace astonishes me again and again.

What amazes me is not the evil in the world. The nightly news has calloused my conscience and hardened my heart. I expect politicians to lie, preachers to have affairs, and doctors to amputate the wrong leg. Television has taken me places I did not want to go. I have become so cynical that I can watch children starving in Ethiopia while I eat my dinner.

What I find encouraging is that evil has been unable to overcome goodness and grace. Benny's request that we pray for the men who beat him is testimony to the triumph of grace. Evil has not been utterly defeated. One look at Benny's face makes such sentimentality naive. Yet his gracious response also testifies to evil's inability to destroy grace.

Russian writer Vasily Grossman wrote,

> Human history is not the battle of good strug-
> gling to overcome evil. It is a battle fought by
> a great evil struggling to crush a small kernel
> of human kindness. But if what is human in
> human beings has not been destroyed even now,
> then evil will never conquer.[8]

I consider this kernel of human kindness to be the
reflection of divine love. It is what Quakers call the
Inner Light, the guiding presence of God within us that
can never be extinguished.

Paul wrote, "Do not be overcome by evil, but overcome evil with good" (Romans 12:21). This is the ethic of
Jesus, of Gandhi, of Dr. Martin Luther King Jr., of
Mother Teresa, and of countless others. It is an ethic that
makes sense only if the grace of God will ultimately triumph. If evil and sin ultimately determine nothing, they
can be mocked. We are freed to meet evil with grace
even when evil would kill us.

Some might suggest that if Benny had died I would
not have experienced the triumph of grace in that emergency room. They are probably right. But knowing
Benny's rich and deep faith in God, I suspect I would
have experienced it at his funeral. I would have been re-

minded of his grace and challenged to emulate him. I might even have been able to pray for his murderers.

At his funeral, I would have reminded us that death is not the final word. "When the perishable has been clothed with the imperishable, and the mortal with immortality, then the saying that is written will come true; 'Death has been swallowed up in victory'" (1 Corinthians 15:54). We need not despair.

This fearless approach to death changes our perspective on life. We can abandon our insecurities. We can risk everything we have. We can develop our strengths as we accept our weaknesses. This certainty in the grace of God has empowered people of faith to face lions in coliseums, crosses on hills, and fiery stakes. The martyr's joy bears witness to the triumph of grace.

This is not to deny the real power of evil. Those who have not discovered the grace of God are especially vulnerable to evil's continued aggression, but none of us is immune from attack. This is precisely why the good news of the resurrection needs to be proclaimed. God's grace, while offered eternally, is available immediately. Evil and sin need not reign a single additional day in our lives.

One woman, when she heard of my belief in the salvation of all people, demanded, "If you're right, why should we evangelize? They'll all make it eventually."

Her question saddened me. It is the misery of millions right now, not their ultimate destiny, that motivates me. I answered, "What better message is there than God's love for every person? What better motivation to spread this good news than the evil and misery that still plague our world?"

Though I believe all will be saved, I greet each morning hoping this will be the day of salvation—when wars cease, famines end, hate turns to love, and every person sees every other person as a child of God. So I spread the good news of this grace. I work for the salvation of the world. My hope is that the more we live in this grace, the less sin can cling to our hearts. The more of us who know this grace, the less evil can do in our world.

The triumph of grace is not complete. It cannot be complete until every last person has been redeemed. Some are experiencing redemption in this life. Some will experience it after their death. But grace will triumph.

I find much of the Revelation of John incomprehensible. Most who preach from it emphasize its violence and wrath. But there is one passage that sings the grace of God. John describes a new heaven and a new earth. He tells of the Holy City. He hears the voice of God saying, "Now the dwelling of God is with men, and he will live with them. They will be his people, and God himself will be with them and be their God. He will wipe every tear from their eyes. There will be no more death or mourning or crying or pain, for the old order of things will pass away" (Revelation 21:3–4).

I can hear that voice.

It is the voice of God proclaiming the triumph of grace.

Forever and for everyone.

1. Thomas Talbott, *The Inescapable Love of God* (Parkland, FL: Universal Publishers, 1999), 102. Talbott makes a convincing argument for the corrective nature of divine punishment.

2. C. S. Lewis, *The Great Divorce* (New York: Simon and Schuster, 1996), 33. Though Lewis never adopted universalism, this little book certainly suggests he gave it serious consideration.

3. Lewis, *Great Divorce,* 36.

4. William Barclay, *The Gospel of Matthew* (Philadelphia: Westminster Press, 1975), 193.

5. Frederick Craddock, *Luke* (Louisville, KY: John Knox Press, 1990), 185.

6. Clarence Jordan, *The Substance of Faith* (New York: Association Press, 1972), 148.

7. David Lowes Watson, *God Does Not Foreclose: The Universal Promise of Salvation* (Nashville: Abingdon, 1990), 65. Watson argues only universalism can save Christianity from becoming irrelevant.

8. Vasily Grossman, *Life and Fate* (New York: Harper and Row, 1980), 410. This is a beautiful novel exploring many questions of life and religion within the context of World War II.

A p p e n d i x   1

Universalist Themes and Verses in Scripture

Introduction

I believe our experiences with God can be trusted. This doesn't mean the Bible should be ignored. Thomas Talbott, in his book *The Inescapable Love of God,* argues that the New Testament is universalist. Though I find many of his interpretations of Scripture enlightening, I remain unconvinced. I believe the early church was as liable to diminish the grace of God as the church today.

The Scriptures listed below are not intended to be proof that the Bible, Jesus, or Paul believed all would be saved. I don't know. I do know there are biblical themes, stories, and verses that imply the salvation of all. These Scriptures have been ignored or discounted by most of

Christianity. Commentaries insist they can't mean what they say.

Since I don't believe the Bible inerrant, I have no need either to harmonize every voice or to explain away every inconsistency. I am willing and able to say of many verses, "I don't believe that to be true." But I'm also excited the Bible isn't unanimous about the destiny of humanity. There are minority voices. Though some of them represent a Christocentric view, they all call into question the damnation of God's children.

I encourage those of you convinced the Bible is the inerrant word of God to examine and study these verses. You may remain unconvinced, but you can't ignore what you claim is without error. For those less committed to biblical authority, I hope these verses allow you to reclaim a book full of truth.

Hebrew Scripture

All peoples on earth will be blessed through you.
Genesis 12:3

I will have mercy on whom I have mercy, and I will have compassion on whom I will have compassion.
Exodus 33:19

I know that you can do all things; no plan of yours can
be thwarted.

Job 42:2

All the ends of the earth will remember and turn to the
Lord, and all the families of the nations will bow down
before him.

Psalm 22:27

Praise awaits you, O God, in Zion; to you our vows will
be fulfilled. O you who hear prayer, to you all men will
come.

Psalm 65:1–2

Where can I go from your Spirit? Where can I flee
from your presence? If I go up to the heavens, you are
there; if I make my bed in the depths [*sheol*], you are
there.

Psalm 139:7–8

The Lord is gracious and compassionate, slow to anger
and rich in love. The Lord is good to all; he has
compassion on all he has made. All you have made will
praise you, O Lord.

Psalm 145:8–10

On this mountain the Lord Almighty will prepare a feast of rich food for all peoples, a banquet of aged wine—the best of meats and finest of wines. On this mountain he will destroy the shroud that enfolds all peoples, the sheet that covers all nations; he will swallow up death forever. The Sovereign Lord will wipe away tears from all faces; he will remove the disgrace of his people from all the earth.

Isaiah 25:6–8

Turn to me and be saved, all you ends of the earth; for I am God, and there is no other. By myself I have sworn, my mouth has uttered in all integrity a word that will not be revoked. Before me every knee will bow; by me every tongue will swear. They will say of me, "In the Lord alone are righteousness and strength."

Isaiah 45:22–24

It is too small a thing for you to be my servant, to restore the tribes of Jacob and bring back those of Israel I have kept. I will make you a light for the Gentiles, that you may bring my salvation to the end of the earth.

Isaiah 49:6

"This is the covenant I will make with the house of Israel after that time," declares the Lord. "I will put my law in their minds and write it on their hearts. I will be their God and they will be my people. No longer will a man teach his neighbor, or a man his brother, saying, 'Know the Lord,' because they will all know me, from the least of them to the greatest," declares the Lord. "For I will forgive their wickedness and will remember their sins no more."

Jeremiah 31:33–34

I will not carry out my fierce anger, nor will I turn and devastate Ephraim. For I am God, and not man—the Holy One among you. I will not come in wrath.

Hosea 11:9

I will pour out my Spirit on all people. Your sons and daughters will prophesy, your old men dream dreams, your young men will see visions.

Joel 2:28

Then will I purify the lips of the peoples, that all of them may call on the name of the Lord and serve him shoulder to shoulder.

Zephaniah 3:9

Shout and be glad, O Daughter of Zion. For I am coming, and I will live among you. Many nations will be joined with the Lord in that day and will become my people.

> Zechariah 2:10–11

Christian Scripture

Love your enemies and pray for those who persecute you, that you may be sons of your Father in heaven.

> Matthew 5:44–45

I say to you that many will come from the east and the west, and will take their places at the feast with Abraham, Isaac, and Jacob in the kingdom of heaven.

> Matthew 8:11

Whoever does the will of my Father in heaven is my brother and sister and mother.

> Matthew 12:50

Your Father in heaven is not willing that any of these little ones should be lost.

> Matthew 18:14

My house shall be called a house of prayer for all nations.

Mark 11:17

All mankind will see God's salvation.

Luke 3:6

Suppose one of you has a hundred sheep and loses one of them. Does he not leave the ninety-nine in the open country and go after the lost sheep until he finds it?

Luke 15:4

Suppose a woman has ten silver coins and loses one. Does she not light a lamp, sweep the house and search carefully until she finds it?

Luke 15:8

The Son of Man came to seek and save what was lost.

Luke 19:10

The true light that gives light to every man was coming into the world.

John 1:9

God did not send his Son into the world to condemn the world, but to save the world through him.

John 3:17

A time is coming and has now come when true worshipers will worship the Father in spirit and truth, for they are the kind of worshipers the Father seeks.

John 4:23

I have other sheep that are not of this sheep pen. I must bring them also. They too will listen to my voice, and there shall be one flock and one shepherd.

John 10:16

When I am lifted up, I will draw all men to myself.

John 12:32

I did not come to judge the world, but to save it.

John 12:47

You did not choose me, but I chose you.

John 15:16

He [Christ] must remain in heaven until the time comes for God to restore everything, as he promised long ago through his holy prophets.

Acts 3:21

I now realize how true it is that God does not show favoritism, but accepts men from every nation who fear him and do what is right.

Acts 10:34–35

All have sinned and fall short of the glory of God, and are justified freely by his grace through the redemption that came by Christ Jesus.

Romans 3:23–24

Just as the result of one trespass was condemnation for all men, so also the result of one act of righteousness was justification that brings life to all men.

Romans 5:18

I am convinced that neither death nor life, neither angels nor demons, neither the present nor the future, nor any powers, neither height nor depth, nor anything in all of creation, will be able to separate us from the love of God that is in Christ Jesus our Lord.

Romans 8:38–39

God has bound all men over to disobedience so that he may have mercy on all men.

Romans 11:32

Love is patient, love is kind. It does not envy, it does not boast, it is not proud. It is not rude, it is not self-seeking, it is not easily angered, it keeps no record of wrongs. Love does not delight in evil, but rejoices in the truth. It always protects, always hopes, always perseveres. Love never fails.

1 Corinthians 13:4–8

For as in Adam all die, so in Christ all will be made alive.

1 Corinthians 15:22

He made known to us the mystery of his will according to his good pleasure, which he purposed in Christ, to be put into effect when the times will have reached their fulfillment—to bring all things in heaven and on earth together under one head, even Christ.

Ephesians 1:9–10

At the name of Jesus every knee should bow, in heaven and on earth and under the earth, and every tongue confess that Jesus Christ is Lord, to the glory of God the Father.

Philippians 2:10–11

For God was pleased to have all his fullness dwell in him, and through him to reconcile to himself all things, whether things on earth or things in heaven, by making peace through his blood, shed on the cross.

Colossians 1:19–20

For that very reason I was shown mercy so that in me, the worst of sinners, Christ Jesus might display his unlimited patience as an example for those who believe on him and receive eternal life.

1 Timothy 1:16

This is good and pleases God our Savior, who wants all men to be saved and to come to a knowledge of the truth.

1 Timothy 2:3–4

This is a trustworthy saying that deserves full acceptance, and for this we labor and strive, that we have put our hope in the living God, who is the Savior of all men, and especially of those who believe.

1 Timothy 4:9–10

For the grace of God that brings salvation has appeared to all men.

Titus 2:11

The Lord is not slow in keeping his promise, as some understand slowness. He is patient with you, not wanting anyone to perish, but everyone to come to repentance.

2 Peter 3:9

Then I heard every creature in heaven and on earth and under the earth and on the sea, and all that is in them, singing, "To him who sits on the throne and to the Lamb be praise and honor and glory and power for ever and ever."

Revelation 5:13

On no day will its [heaven's] gates be shut, for there will be no night there.

Revelation 21:25

A Short History of Universalism

Introduction

I believe our experiences with God can be trusted. This doesn't mean I don't seek confirmation in the experiences of others. I was pleasantly surprised by how many men and women throughout the ages have questioned what I've questioned and thought what I've thought. I was disappointed to discover how often they were persecuted and sometimes killed. Origen was branded a heretic over two hundred years after his death. Thankfully, we live in a day when thinking differently isn't as dangerous.

The quotes below are a few of the many I encountered in writing this book. I offer them not as proof that I'm right, but rather as an indication that I'm in good company. I offer them recognizing that not all these people understood universalism as I do. In addition, not all were consistent in their position. Some considered it a possibility, and others held it as a conviction. Regardless, each quote demonstrates the persistent testimony to the triumph of grace.

The Early Church

There is strong evidence that many in the early church believed in the salvation of every person. This view was not initially thought to be unreasonable, unscriptural, or heretical. J. W. Hanson published a book titled *A Cloud of Witnesses* in 1885 in which he carefully outlined the support and opposition to universalism during the first five centuries of church history. He suggests many early church fathers assumed Christ had died for all, therefore all would be saved. Alexandria, the premier religious school in the East, had several headmasters and teachers who argued for the salvation of every person.

If in this life there are so many ways for purification and

repentance, how much more should there be after death! The purification of souls, when separated from the body, will be easier. We can set no limits to the agency of the Redeemer; to redeem, to rescue, to discipline, is his work, and so will he continue to operate after this life.

Clement, 150–220

We assert that the Word, who is the Wisdom of God, shall bring together all intelligent creatures, and convert them into his own perfection, through the instrumentality of their free will and of their own exertions. The Word is more powerful than all the diseases of the soul, and he applies his remedies to each one according to the pleasure of God—for the name of God is to be invoked by all, so that all shall serve him with one consent.

Origen, 185–254

In the liberation of all no one remains a captive; at the time of the Lord's passion, he alone [the devil] was injured, who lost all the captives he was keeping.

Didymus, 309–395

The Eastern Influence

These voices were not alone. Many in the East would support this position during the many debates and councils. Indeed, this tradition was so strong that the Eastern Orthodox Church never completely abandoned the hope of universal salvation.

For the wicked there are punishments, not perpetual, however, lest the immortality prepared for them should be a disadvantage, but they are to be purified for a brief period according to the amount of malice in their works. They shall therefore suffer punishment for a short space, but immortal blessedness having no end awaits them. . . . The penalties to be inflicted for their many and grave sins are very far surpassed by the magnitude of the mercy to be showed them.

> Diodore of Tarsus,
> 320–394

The process of healing shall be proportioned to the measure of evil in each of us, and when the evil is purged and blotted out, there shall come in each place to each immortality and life and honor.

> Macrina, 327–379

Let them, if they will, walk in our way and in Christ's. If not, let them walk in their own way. Perchance there they will be baptized with fire, with that last, that more laborious and longer baptism, which devours the substance like hay, and consumes the lightness of all evil.

> Gregory of Nazianzus,
> 330–390

In the end and consummation of the Universe all are to be restored into their original harmonious state, and we all shall be made one body and be united once more into a perfect man, and the prayer of our Savior shall be fulfilled that all may be one.

> St. Jerome, 331–420

For it is evident that God will in truth be "in all" when there shall be no evil in existence, when every created being is at harmony with itself, and every tongue shall confess that Jesus Christ is Lord; when every creature shall have been made one body. Now the body of Christ, as I have often said, is the whole of humanity. . . . Participation in bliss awaits everyone.

> St. Gregory of Nyssa,
> 335–390

The wicked who have committed evil the whole period of their lives shall be punished till they learn that, by continuing in sin, they only continue in misery. And when, by this means, they shall have been brought to fear God, and to regard him with good will, they shall obtain the enjoyment of his grace.

Theodore of Mopsuestia,
350–428

In the present life God is in all, for his nature is without limits, but is not all in all. But in the coming life, when mortality is at an end and immortality granted, and sin has no longer any place, God will be all in all. For the Lord, who loves man, punishes medicinally, that he may check the course of impiety.

Theodoret the Blessed,
387–458

That in the world to come, those who have done evil all their life long, will be made worthy of the sweetness of the divine bounty. For never would Christ have said, "Until thou has paid the uttermost farthing" unless it were possible for us to be cleansed when we have paid the debt.

Peter Chrysologus, 435

Without doubt even in the demonic depths the creature remains the work of God and the traits of divine design are never effaced. The image of God, obscured by the infidelity of sin, is nevertheless preserved intact, and that is why there is always, even in the abyss, an ontological receptacle for divine appeal, for the grace of God.

> Father Georges
> Florovsky, Eastern
> Orthodox theologian

Widespread Recognition

Even those who did not hold to the universalist position recognized both its popularity and significance.

The mass of men say that there is to be an end of punishment to those who are punished.

> St. Basil the Great,
> 329–379

There are very many who though not denying the Holy Scriptures, do not believe in endless torments.

> Augustine, 354–430

Becoming Heresy

Augustine would soon become the chief opponent of universalism. He, through the dominance of the Roman Church, would win the day. Universalism became heresy. This would lead to a rejection of many of the early Church Fathers. Origen's theology was declared heretical at the fifth ecumenical council in 553.

The Dark Ages

For nearly a thousand years, theological debate of any kind largely disappeared. Thomas Cahill makes a strong argument in his book, *How the Irish Saved Civilization,* for Ireland as the single locale of significant theological thought. John Scotus (810–877), an Irish theologian, was a strong advocate of universalism and one of the few bright lights in this dark time.

The Reformation

The schism within the Catholic Church that we now call the Reformation was not merely about Luther. It was about many people seeking the freedom to express new ideas. Many of the rebellious groups, the Anabaptists and Quakers, considered the salvation of all as a distinct possibility.

Since love in him was perfect and since love hates or is envious of none, but includes everyone, even though we were all his enemies, surely he would not wish to exclude anyone. And if he had excluded anyone, then love would have been squint-eyed and a respecter of persons. And that, God is not!

Hans Denck, 1495–1527

The humble, meek, merciful, just, pious, and devout souls are everywhere of one religion; and when death has taken off the mask they will know one another, though the diverse liveries they wear here makes them strangers.

William Penn,
1644–1718

Every man has a measure of true and saving grace—the mere measure of light, as it is given to reprove and call him to righteousness. So has God likewise poured forth into the hearts of all men a measure of that divine Light and seed, that, thereby reaching into the consciences of all, He may raise them up out of death and darkness by His life and light.

Robert Barclay,
1648–1690

American Universalism

Universalism became a strong movement in America during the eighteenth century. Dr. George de Benneville in Pennsylvania and the Reverend John Murray in New England were prominent advocates of the salvation of all. Hosea Ballou formulated much of the early Universalist theology in America. Many famous Americans found this theology compelling. Thomas Jefferson and John Quincy Adams both attended Universalist churches.

Go out into the highways and byways. Give the people something of your new vision. You may possess a small light, but uncover it, let it shine, use it in order to bring more light and understanding to the hearts and minds of men and women. Give them not hell but hope and courage; preach the kindness and the everlasting love of God.

John Murray, 1741–1815

The Universal doctrine prevails more and more in our country, particularly among persons eminent for their piety, in whom it is not a mere speculation but a principle of action in the heart prompting to practical goodness.

Benjamin Rush,
1745–1813

As to the justice of endless punishment, minds enjoying the liberty of free inquiry could easily detect the diabolical character of such justice, as it is the exact opposite of the Divine nature, which is love. Such justice is evidently predicated on the false principle and ungodly practice of rendering evil for evil.

Hosea Ballou, 1771–1852

The belief that the great Jehovah was offended with his creatures to that degree that nothing but the death of Christ, or the endless misery of mankind, could appease his anger, is an idea that has done more injury to the Christian religion than . . . the writings of all its opposers, for many centuries. The error has been fatal to the life and spirit of the religion of Christ in our world. All those principles which are to be dreaded by men, have been believed to exist in God, and professors have been moulded into the image of their Deity, and become more cruel than them. . . .

> Hosea Ballou

Universalism is the most beautiful word in the English language.

> Elizabeth Barrett
> Browning, 1806–1861

If I were Christ, nothing could satisfy me but that every human being should in the end be saved, and therefore I am sure that nothing less will satisfy Him.

> Hannah Whitehall
> Smith, 1870

Modern Universalists

Many today believe the salvation of all to be both Christian and compelling.

The only victory love can enjoy is the day when its offer of love is answered by the return of love. The only possible final triumph is a universe loved by and in love with God.

William Barclay

A theology of grace implies universal salvation. What could grace mean if it were granted only to some sinners and not to others according to an arbitrary decree that is totally contrary to the nature of God? If grace is granted according to the greater or lesser number of sins, it is no longer grace.

Jacques Ellul

All will be redeemed in God's fullness of time, all, not just the small portion of the population who have been given the grace to know and accept Christ. All the strayed and stolen sheep. All the little lost ones.

Madeleine L'Engle

Only when we see that we are part of the totality of the planet, not a superior part with special privileges, can we work effectively to bring about an earth restored to wholeness.

Elizabeth Watson

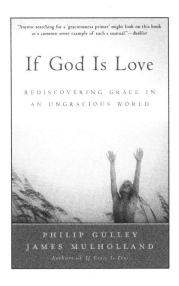

Plus:

Plus: Insights, Interviews, and More

Plus:

Afterword

The idea for this book was born in the early years of my pastoral ministry, while studying theology at Marian College in Indianapolis. Appalled at the apparent ease with which traditional Christianity consigned billions of people to eternal punishment, I remarked to my professor, John Lowe, that such beliefs seemed contrary to the God I'd experienced. "If I were God," I said, "I would not be happy unless I were reconciled with all my children."

"Then you might be a universalist," he said cheerfully, as if that were an admirable theological condition.

After class, I traipsed across campus to the library and there discovered Clement, Origen, and other early Christians who could not bring themselves to believe God's final word to anyone would be a word of condemnation. I began identifying myself as a universalist, believing if there were a God worthy of worship and emulation, that God would be unswervingly devoted to the eternal well-being of all people everywhere.

During the next several years, I shared this insight in sermons, to mixed reviews. One congregation fired me, but another congregation was receptive, urging me to develop my thoughts. More years passed and I was writing books that were enjoying wide readership, so began to entertain the idea of writing, with Jim Mulholland, a book about universalism. My publisher at the time, a conservative Christian, was less than enthusiastic and terminated my writing contracts. Soon after, HarperCollins invited me to work with them, and I accepted, with the understanding they would publish this book.

A year before *If Grace Is True* was published, the *Indianapolis Star** ran a lengthy article about the forth-

---

* *The Indianapolis Star,* January 26, 2002, p. F1.

coming book under the headline "Grace Under Fire." It would prove to be a prophetic heading. Within days, letters demanding the rescinding of my recording (ordination) were circulating among the Quaker meetings in my area. Because my superintendent was sympathetic to theological diversity, the efforts to defrock me gained little traction. This would change when more traditional superintendents assumed that position and lent their support to the effort to rescind my recording. At this writing, in mid 2009, it remains to be seen whether I will retain my pastoral credentials in a denomination famous for its tolerance.

. . . it remains to be seen whether I will retain my pastoral credentials in a denomination famous for its tolerance.

The story of this book is the story of other ironies—a death threat against my family and me signed "In Christian Love." The writer of that cheerful missive lived two thousand miles away in California, so I didn't worry, but was struck, and remain so, at the jarring inconsistency of a letter calling for my family's death ending on such a high and gracious note.

I have grown accustomed to persons not shaking my hand, crossing the street at my approach, targeting my children for conversion, demanding my ouster from the pastoral ministry, and insisting I repent, simply for believing in grace and its logical implications. I recall an incident when a lady accosted me, shaking with anger and indignation, condemning me to hell. (I'm amazed by the number of people who think threatening someone with hell who doesn't believe in it will be a deterrent.) Then there was the man in Lincoln, Nebraska who protested an appearance Jim and I were making at a local church. He was holding an eight-foot cross and yelling at persons as they entered the church. Jim wanted to engage the man and win him over, but I saw in the man's eye the gleam of fanaticism, envisioned Jim getting thumped upside the head with a big cross, and advised my friend against it.

What has been far more rewarding, and even more memorable, are the hundreds of letters we've received from people whose lives have been transformed by this book. I remember one in particular, from a mother who'd been estranged from her lesbian daughter for a number of years. After reading *If Grace Is True,* the mother saw her daughter in a new light, called her child to seek forgiveness, and the two were happily reconciled. A letter like that beats a royalty check hands down.

Every now and then, a pastor will write to say he or she embraced this belief in radical grace, only to be fired when they shared their convictions aloud. Were I to rewrite this book, I would include a word of caution to pastors to proceed cautiously, that many people do not receive word of God's unlimited grace as good news. But occasionally we will hear from a pastor who dared to speak of such inclusive love and found their words fell on open hearts and minds. They'll tell about changed lives, of renewed churches, of divisions healed. I used to be surprised by such letters, but have come to understand that is what grace does.

Whenever Jim and I speak, it is our custom to invite questions from listeners. They often ask what it was like writing a book together. (Enjoyable, but slow. This book took four years to write. The fifth chapter took an entire year.) They want to know what we think about Jesus. (We think well of Jesus, but sus-

> *Were I to rewrite this book, I would include a word of caution to pastors to proceed cautiously, that many people do not receive word of God's unlimited grace as good news.*

pect the church has made claims about Jesus that as a first-century, monotheistic Jew he wouldn't have made about himself.) Sometimes we're asked if our Quaker meetings fired us for writing this book. (We made sure they knew what we believed before they employed us. If we ever get fired, it will be for other reasons.) By far, the most frequent question we hear is, "Where can I find a church that believes these things?" Our response is always the same, "Keep looking. If you can't find one, start one. But don't name it after us." For the purpose of this book wasn't to gain followers, but to help people think about an amazing grace most Christians happily sing about, but whose consequences they rarely consider.

I hope the experience of reading *If Grace Is True* helped you see grace in a new light.

Summer 2009
Philip Gulley

Discussion Questions

Chapter One—The Dilemma

1. Do our theological formulas keep us from being gracious to the "Sallys" of the world, whose life experiences make it difficult for them to believe in a loving God?

2. I had a friend who once observed about another person, "He's a better man than his theology." Do you believe one's religious beliefs could make him crueler than he would otherwise be?

3. Are there instances when we might be more gracious than God? If so, what does that say about our understanding of God?

Chapter Two—Trusting Our Experience with God

1. Can you think of any revelation from God that has ever happened apart from your or someone else's personal experience of God?

2. Why do you think some people are reluctant to believe their personal experiences of God are trustworthy?

3. Do you believe some people's experiences of God are more valid than other people's experiences? Why or why not?

Chapter Three—The Character of God

1. Has your understanding of God changed over the course of your life? If so, what prompted those changes?

2. If God is love, is it appropriate to reject any understanding of God that isn't ultimately loving and gracious?

3. Can our understanding of what constitutes holiness
   cause us to be ungracious at times?

Chapter Four—The Will of God

1. What do you believe is the primary will of God?

2. Do you believe God is the cause of every act?

3. Do you believe God is free to reject our rejection?
   What might that mean?

4. Is it possible to "wear out" God's patience?

Chapter Five—The Salvation of God

1. What does it mean to be saved?

2. Do you think God required the spilling of blood in
   order to save anyone? Why or why not?

3. Does it undermine Christianity if we no longer speak
   of Jesus as the sacrifice made on our behalf to appease God's wrath?

4. How else might we understand the crucifixion and
   the role of Jesus?

Chapter Six—The Persistence of God

1. As a child, who were you told was going to hell?
   Why? Do you believe that?

2. Do you believe death is the final word, or can God's
   love transcend the grave?

Plus: Insights, Interviews, and More

3. Who do you imagine will be seated next to you at the Great Banquet?

4. Who do you need to forgive? What keeps you from that?

5. From whom do you need to seek forgiveness? What keeps you from that?

Introduction from *If the Church Were Christian*

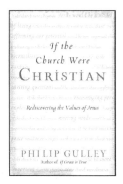

An excerpt from the latest book by Philip Gulley

When I was seven years old and preparing for my first communion, the teacher explained the illustrious history of our church— our miraculous beginnings, those seasons of peril when God intervened to preserve us, the heroic figures who led our church through the wilderness, the glorious conviction that our church alone had remained faithful to Jesus's vision. Naturally, I was grateful I'd been born into the one true church.*

While I was delighted at my good fortune, I worried about my father's family, who generations before had allied themselves with an apostate movement. We were regularly encouraged to pray for those who belonged to "lesser" churches. Jesus spoke of such people, those who said "Lord, Lord," but wouldn't enter the kingdom of heaven. He was talking, I was certain, about my relatives.

When I was a teenager, I was discussing religion with a friend who belonged to another denomination. I was surprised to discover that his church had the same vaunted history as mine. They, too, were uniquely chosen and blessed by God. They, too, traced their lineage

---

* The word church has sometimes been capitalized when referring to the universal church—the Church. It conveys a sense of privilege and entitlement this Quaker increasingly rejects. In the interests of ecclesial modesty, I have elected not to do that in this book, believing it confers a status not always merited. In my mind, such grammatical tributes should be earned, not demanded.

Plus: Insights, Interviews, and More

to Jesus. They, too, were obedient to God's Word. They, too, remained uniquely pure, untainted by the world. They, too, were praying—but for me.

Initially, I found this unsettling. I wasn't sure which one of us was deceived. Given the nature of exclusive claims, one of us had to be wrong. My friend's certainty seemed so complete, it caused me to doubt mine. I began to suspect I'd been misled, and when he urged me to visit his church, I went. Within a year, I'd joined his Quaker meeting, convinced I'd discovered the real thing.

In my adult years, I began to wonder if the language of ecclesiastical purity, such as "the One True Church" and "the Reformed Church," was based on a faulty assumption—that we can actually know what Jesus intended the church to be. Whether our arguments for spiritual supremacy relied on an unbroken chain of apostolic succession, a literal reading of an inerrant Bible, or an insight gained in a moment of spiritual enlightenment, we all claimed to know the heart and mind of Jesus and his hope for the church, despite little evidence that Jesus even gave the church much thought. Most of what we assert about the church is based on fragmentary hints from Jesus and two thousand years of tradition.

Several years ago I visited a museum and saw the skeleton of a dinosaur. As I read the plaque, I learned only a handful of the bones were original, that the remainder had been fabricated based on a paleontologist's extrapolation from the authentic bones. In many ways, this is similar to what the church has done. There are only two passages in one gospel (Matthew 16:18 and 18:17) where Jesus mentions the church, and even those references are dubious. Many scholars suspect the Matthean verses were not original to Jesus but were written back into the text by persons hoping to bolster their theological and ecclesial positions by placing them in the mouth of Jesus. From those two verses, we have built a vast institution based on these "hints" Jesus gave us. But we should never delude ourselves into thinking that today's church sprang directly from the mind and witness of Jesus. All we have is extrapolation, a few bones upon which have been erected a larger organism.

If Jesus intended to create the church, he did a questionable job. He left no clear directions about its structure or purpose. The apostle Paul and others would later do that, but Jesus didn't. Jesus did no fund-raising. In fact, he seemed unconcerned about financial development, telling his disciples to take no money for their ministry. If the disciples were his first board of directors, he chose poorly. In their first major decision, replacing Judas, they shunned standard business practices and drew lots.

A fair reading of the earliest gospels offers scant evidence that Jesus intended to start a new religion.

Jesus did none of the things essential to forming a viable institution. Some may argue that Jesus wasn't negligent, that he was simply confident in the Holy Spirit's ability to guide and grow the fledging church. But Jesus's cautionary, even hostile, language about religious institutions makes such a claim doubtful, if not incredible. A fair reading of the earliest gospels offers scant evidence that Jesus intended to start a new religion.

Though a convincing argument could be made that Jesus didn't found the church, it seems unlikely that present-day Christians will disband their congregations. For many of us, it's difficult to imagine a world without the church. Even if Jesus didn't intend to start the church, it will likely endure in one form or another. But if the church claims Jesus as its founder, it should at least share his values. The question for Christians is whether the church reflects the priorities of Jesus.

This question has divided the church again and again. There are roughly 39,000 Christian denominations, each of which has a slightly different take on the priorities of Jesus.* All denominations, whether liberal or conservative, share the conviction that they most faithfully follow Jesus. They earnestly believe Jesus imagined the church as looking just like them. When I became a Quaker, I sincerely believed Jesus had been raised in an early version of a Quaker meetinghouse.

The era of uncritical acceptance of Jesus stories is past and with it the church's claim to a divinely ordained status.

It seems arrogant for any of us to suggest that we alone have most accurately discerned the true intentions of Jesus. This is always the great temptation. After I wrote my books on universal salvation,** I was often approached by persons urging me to start a new denomination. They believed my opinion of a specific theological doctrine was an adequate foundation for a new institution. I declined their invitations for three reasons: I found community with my own church satisfying; I had no confidence in my ability to create a pure Christianity after thirty-nine thousand denominations had tried and failed; and I feared that being a key figure in a new movement would expand my head and shrink my heart.

In addition to the growing diversity of the Christian faith, there has been an explosion of knowledge in the past hundred years about the Bible and its formation. While this has broadened our understanding of

---

* According to the Gordon-Conwell Theological Seminary's "Status of Global Mission, 2008" report, there are now over thirty-nine thousand Christian denominations in the world.

** *If Grace Is True* and *If God Is Love*, both published by HarperOne, and cowritten with James Mulholland.

Jesus and his culture, it has also cast doubt on what the church had always assumed were the authentic sayings and activities of Jesus. The era of uncritical acceptance of Jesus stories is past and with it the church's claim to a divinely ordained status.

Gone also is the clear blueprint for Christian conduct we assumed Matthew, Mark, Luke, and John offered. The gospel accounts, written some thirty to sixty years after the death of Jesus, are the early church's words about Jesus, not necessarily the actual words of Jesus. So to even say, "Jesus said this," or "Jesus said that" is to make an assumption that might not be true.

Nevertheless, the story of Jesus is a compelling one and still has the power to shape, form, and transform our lives. We can just no longer assume there is universal agreement on what that story means, if ever we could. Nor can we assume that the gospel versions of the Jesus story are historically accurate. The lessons might well be existentially true—that is, they possess a spiritual richness and value—but to claim they are historically accurate is likely an overstatement and a misunderstanding of their genre and purpose.

All of these developments—the staggering number of denominations, the rise of biblical criticism, and the diminishing authority of the church and the Bible— have made it impossible to articulate a universal understanding of what it means to be Christian. This should not deter us from offering our particular understanding of Christianity, so long as we bear in mind we are speaking from our own experience and our experience is always limited.

Though beliefs within Christendom vary, and the chance for universal consensus slim, we still must think creatively about what it means to be Christian and what we mean when we say the church is

Christian, even though that description will grow outdated. For it is also clear that what it means to be Christian has changed dramatically over the centuries and will continue to change. The "old-time religion" of which some still sing is a relatively new-time religion, not "good enough for the Hebrew children," not even recognizable to them.

Even as the understanding of what it means to be Christian has shifted, so has the word itself. We speak of "doing our Christian duty" and by that mean doing what we believe to be virtuous and good, apart from any specific belief about Jesus. Whatever the word *Christianity* might have meant at one time, it now means—to many, many people—being nice.

A woman once phoned, asking if I could officiate at her wedding. Some pastors have strict theological criteria about whom they will marry. While I don't, before I could even explain my protocol, the woman hastened to inform me she was Christian.

"Oh, what church do you attend?" I asked.

"I've never really gone to church," she said.

If I had been defining Christianity strictly by one's participation in a Christian community, she would not have been Christian. But I hadn't, so our conversation continued.

"Did you mean to say that Jesus is your Savior?" I asked.

"I don't think so," she said.

"What do you mean, then, when you say you're a Christian?" I asked, my curiosity growing.

"I guess what I meant is that my grandmother goes to church and I grew up in America," she said.

So Christianity was something one inherited by virtue of his or her lineage or nationality.

I didn't challenge her definition; I simply remembered it and since then have heard it echoed by others.

The criteria for Christian faith now seems to be this: if I say I am a Christian, I am.

While those who value theological clarity might bristle at such loose terms, the alternative would have us examining one another closely, judging who among us is fit to bear that name, attempting to construct a definition suitable to all, which is both undesirable and impossible.

All of this is to say that the Christian faith I am about to articulate might well satisfy only a church of one. My faith is informed by my experience as a Roman Catholic and a Quaker, by my twenty-five years in pastoral ministry, by the many diverse people I have encountered in my life, and by my growing conviction that Christianity is less a codified doctrine or creed and more an approach to life that emphasizes grace, is always on the side of human dignity, is always devoted to our spiritual growth and moral evolution, and is always committed to the ongoing search for truth, even if that search leads us away from institutional Christianity.

But if history has taught us anything, it is that renewal blossoms in the most unlikely places, perhaps even in the church.

If my hope in this book is the rediscovery of the values of Jesus, it seems odd to suggest the church might not be the vehicle for that regeneration. But if history has taught us anything, it is that renewal blossoms in the most unlikely places, perhaps even in the church. If you've ever been mystified by the activities of some churches, left to wonder what in the world they had to do with the ethic of Jesus, consider this book an invitation to appraise our current priorities and whether they honor the Christian values we claim to cherish.

Such introspection is not always welcomed by the church. For the past several years, there has been a sustained effort to rescind my credentials as a pastor in the Religious Society of Friends. While these efforts have at times been a distraction, they have served to confirm my hunch that any religion whose goal is the exclusion of others is bound to fail, if only because it cannot ignite our imaginations and sustain our spirits.

With these qualifications, and with the ready admission of my own inconsistency in living out these ideals, I offer my thoughts on what the church might look like if it were Christian.